Praise for

ANGEL *in Aisle 3*

"I made a mistake in opening *Angel in Aisle 3*. While waiting for a phone call that didn't come, I decided to read only the first chapter. It's now five hours later and I've wasted most of my working day reading this book . . . Or did I waste it? The inspirational story of two men from completely different walks of life who changed each other's lives kept me turning pages. It reads like an extended parable with snippets of wisdom sprinkled throughout the chapters. After I turned the last page, one thought hit me: I wish I had known Don."

—***Cecil Murphey***, author or coauthor of more than 130 books, including *Gifted Hands: The Ben Carson Story*, and *90 Minutes in Heaven* with Don Piper

"God works in mysterious ways, and Kevin's story is evidence of this. God wants to do more than change us cosmetically—He transforms us from the inside out. An amazing, honest, raw tale of mercy in the midst of life's big struggles."

—***Chris Fabry***, host of the daily program *Chris Fabry Live!* on Moody Radio and author of more than 70 books, including nonfiction, film novelizations, and novels for children and young adult

"Being a filmmaker who has come across many stories, I was mesmerized by this soul-baring account of Kevin and Don. Within a few pages I was swept into a journey I never could have anticipated. This true story is a message of hope for all who read it. I've known Kevin for many years, and have long been thoroughly impressed by his ability to combine wonderfully creative storytelling with important and inspirational themes."

—***Rick Bieber***, writer, director, or producer of over 30 feature films and television/cable movies, including *The 5th Quarter, Crazy, Flatliners, Made in America*, and *Radio Flyer*

"Kevin West's inspirational book will bless the Body of Christ in many ways. His journey from the corporate world to prison to the pastorate is not only heart-rending but very instructional for every follower of Christ. All of us need help toward our destiny and assignments in the Kingdom. In this page-turner, you will be blessed and amazed as you meet Kevin's helpers!"

—***Jim Hodges***, founder, president, and apostolic team leader of the Federation of Ministers and Churches International in Duncanville, Texas

"Pastor Kevin West is an artesian well of wisdom. His insight and sensitivity to the Holy Spirit coupled with his measured but powerful presence encourages bold and visionary leadership."

—***Steve Williams***, Mayor of the City of Huntington, West Virginia

ANGEL *in Aisle 3*

THE TRUE STORY OF
a mysterious vagrant, a convicted bank executive, and the unlikely friendship that saved both their lives

KEVIN WEST

with John Frederick Edwards

HOWARD BOOKS
An Imprint of Simon & Schuster, Inc.
New York Nashville London Toronto Sydney New Delhi

Howard Books
An Imprint of Simon & Schuster, Inc.
1230 Avenue of the Americas
New York, NY 10020

First Howard Books trade paperback edition December 2016

HOWARD and colophon are trademarks of Simon & Schuster, Inc.

For information about special discounts for bulk purchases, please contact Simon & Schuster Special Sales at 1-866-506-1949 or business@simonandschuster.com.

The Simon & Schuster Speakers Bureau can bring authors to your live event. For more information or to book an event, contact the Simon & Schuster Speakers Bureau at 1-866-248-3049 or visit our website at www.simonspeakers.com.

Designed by Davina Mock-Maniscalco

Manufactured in the United States of America

10 9 8 7 6 5 4 3 2 1

Library of Congress Cataloging-in-Publication Data

Names: West, Kevin (Kevin Ray) | Edwards, Frederick.
Title: Angel in aisle 3 : a mysterious vagrant, a convicted bank executive, and the unlikely friendship that saved both their lives / Kevin West, with Frederick Edwards.
Other titles: Angel in aisle three
Description: First Howard Books hardcover edition. | New York : Howard Books, 2015. | "Howard Books non fiction original hardcover"—Title page verso.
Identifiers: LCCN 2015017513 | ISBN 9781476794006 (hardcover) | ISBN 9781476794020 (trade paper) | ISBN 9781476794013 (ebook)
Subjects: LCSH: West, Kevin (Kevin Ray) | Grocers—Ohio—Ironton—Biography. | Tramps—Ohio—Ironton—Biography. | Bankers—Ohio—Ironton—Biography. | First-time offenders—Ohio—Ironton—Biography. | Friendship. | Redemption. | Bible—Study and teaching—Ohio—Ironton. | Christian biography—Ohio—Ironton. | Ironton (Ohio)—Biography.
Classification: LCC F499.176 W37 2015 | DDC 270.092—dc23
LC record available at http://lccn.loc.gov/2015017513

ISBN 978-1-4767-9400-6
ISBN 978-1-4767-9402-0 (pbk)
ISBN 978-1-4767-9401-3 (ebook)

To Leesa, my precious wife and best friend.
And to my daughters, Lauren, Lindsey, and Lakyn; my son, Kaiden;
my granddaughters, Braylie and Aubree; and my son-in-law, Bradley—
the joys of my life.

CHAPTER

One

He said his name was Don and that he needed some groceries. And he called me "son."

"Son," he said, "can I get a little credit until the first of the month? Maybe twenty dollars for some lunchmeat and milk?" He was an elderly man—seventy or so. His stained khakis were too short and were secured by a frayed leather belt. He wore brown shoes held together with knotted laces. The left sleeve of his soiled shirt was torn, and a button was missing from the front. He had a long, matted beard and greasy gray hair. And he reeked with body odor.

"Sure," I said. "Twenty dollars is fine."

How could I know that this untidy man before me would change my life forever? When I described him to some friends in my Bible study group, they didn't believe me. Rather than come out and blatantly accuse me of conjuring him up, they simply implied that I was exaggerating. Surely, in their minds, my mounting stress had created this mysterious stranger. "Maybe he's an angel," one friend said. Wherever Don came from, I knew he was real and not a figment of my imagination. And what he taught me in the coming weeks and months preserved my family and completely transformed my life.

How could I know that this untidy man before me would change my life forever?

At first glance most people would likely have written him off as a homeless panhandler. They wouldn't have looked past his ragged beard and unkempt gray hair as he limped slowly toward them on his bad leg. But from the first day I talked with him, I knew there was much more to this man than what met the eye. What I didn't realize at the time was that God was drawing me into an extraordinary friendship. This unusual stranger came into my life during my darkest period. I was facing imprisonment, my marriage was at the breaking point, and my faith was in shambles.

Late one night in January 1997, only two months before I met Don, I was working at my computer in our home in Ashland, Kentucky, when I was surprised by my wife, Leesa, standing in the doorway. With one arm around our older daughter, Lauren, and holding Lindsey on her hip, she stood silently studying me.

"What is it?" I asked. My words came out too sharply and startled her.

"We just came down to give you a good-night kiss."

I waited for her to bring the girls closer but she didn't move. My harsh tone had changed her mood.

"Kev," she said, "we don't even know who you are anymore." She then turned and left the room with our daughters.

Her words cut right through me. I stood and started to follow her but stopped myself. What could I say? I knew she was right. She didn't know who I was because *I* didn't even know.

I was in deep trouble, the kind of trouble she could never imagine. I had drifted far from my faith. My pursuit of success had driven me to illegal practices at the bank where I was vice president. I had been administering loans to unqualified partners in a land development business, and I was now facing the possibility of getting caught. I didn't know what I was going to do. All the loans I had misappropriated were up for renewal, and I knew I could no longer continue in this mire that I had created.

I sat back down at my computer and tried to work but couldn't. The truth of my wife's words forced me to examine myself. I couldn't believe I had fallen this far. The hunger for success, the drive of ambition had lured me down a dark path. Gradually I had become more detached from my family.

I began pacing back and forth from my office to the living room, agonizing over my predicament. I was cornered, with absolutely no chance of escape. I felt as if I were suffocating. I had no friend or family member who could help me. This whole ordeal was a dark secret that I couldn't share with anyone. The few who did know about it were involved in it too.

It's odd what comes to mind when you've gone completely adrift. I remembered the time my third-grade teacher, Mrs. Bell, told me that the low grade on my exam wasn't like me, that I was much better than that. Her personal attention and persistent conversations with my mother pushed me to excel. I also thought back to my elementary school coach, Frank, who had faith in me despite my clumsiness on the basketball court. I had a hard time managing a basketball, although I was at ease with a football. Coach Frank spent hours training me throughout football season so he could add me to his basketball team in the spring. He told me every day that handling a basketball with skill was no harder than handling a football. He saw potential in me that didn't blossom until two years later when I joined his sixth-grade basketball team. Coach Frank's encouragement ultimately gave me the confidence to succeed later on with high-school sports in ways I had never dreamed.

I also remembered my father's insightful words during my youthful struggles: "When you find yourself in disappointment, it doesn't define you. What matters is how you respond to it." I was far too immature at that time to comprehend the wisdom of his words, but now they came back to me with powerful meaning. How would I respond to my current situation? Would I let it define me, or could I rise above it? I honestly didn't know. I had no clue how to respond.

As I walked back and forth through the living room, I realized for the first time that God, through His grace, had surrounded me with amazing mentors. That night, as I thought about disappointing them, I knew it was not my doing that had drawn those people to me. It was simply God's unearned favor. Every good thing in my life had freely come by the Lord's hand. My pride had blinded me to this truth and had sent me down a dead-end street.

At one point during that long evening I stood at our bay window to watch the onset of a rainstorm. Harsh winds bent thin saplings almost to the ground and snapped rotten limbs off some of the older trees. It was as if God were washing everything clean as an example for me. I looked out for a long time, staring at the rain as it beat against the window, thinking how foreign my actions would seem to my parents and how difficult they would be to understand.

I couldn't bear the thought of telling my father and mother about my wrongdoing. My parents had raised me to love the Lord. They didn't just talk about following Christ; they demonstrated it in all they said and did. I remembered how my mother always found out about families in need and bought extra groceries for them. Early on Saturday mornings while my friends watched cartoons in their pajamas, my father and I would get in our 1975 Chevy Impala and drive through the neighborhoods in Ashland to a home designated by my mother. When we arrived at our destination, I would hop out of the car and secretly leave a bag of food on the doorstep. Taking care of others was always on my parents' hearts. I knew my reckless actions would be an absolute shock to them and would bring them great sadness.

Worst of all, however, was having to tell Leesa. She exemplified all that was tender and right in a wife. She was the virtuous woman described in Proverbs 31 whose children rise up and call her blessed and whose husband safely trusts in her. I deeply loved her and my children and knew they deserved much better than what I had become.

That night as I stood at the window, I remembered my mother saying to me, "When your back is up against the wall, don't run *from* God but run *to* Him."

"When your back is up against the wall, don't run *from* God but run *to* Him."

At one thirty in the morning, having paced and cried for three hours, I called out to God. "Lord, please take this mess from me," I prayed. "I'm giving it to You."

I can't describe exactly what happened at that moment, except to say I was suddenly released from my burden. I knew I had to face the consequences of my wrong, but now I felt safely held in the palm of my Father's hand. The weight had lifted.

What wasn't revealed to me just then was the extraordinary provision the Lord would send me in less than two months.

I sat back down at my computer and typed out my resignation from the bank.

The next day, after resigning from my position at the bank, I came home and told Leesa everything. As I held her in my arms, I explained that I had illegally benefited from loans I had made for my partners in our land development business. At first she didn't believe me—it was beyond her comprehension. When she finally broke into tears, I knew the immensity of her pain was because of her love for me.

"Can you go to prison for this?" she asked.

"Yes, Lee." I knew of this possibility, but admitting it to her almost made me sick. The severity of my misdeeds became all the more clear.

"What will happen then?" she asked.

"I don't know," I said. And I didn't. I had taken every bit of financial security I had created for my family and thrown it to the wind. My good salary and all my benefits were gone. I would likely be in prison soon and completely unable to provide for my family. I didn't know how long I would be incarcerated or how Leesa and the girls would survive. Losing our home seemed certain.

"How will you ever make it in prison?" Leesa asked.

"I don't know yet what's going to happen," I said, trying to give her some kind of answer.

"What about us while you're gone?" she said, crying. "What then?"

I knew that offering any other answer was futile. "I don't know, Lee," I repeated. "I know the Lord is with us now, but other than that, I just don't know."

As a teen, Leesa had faced catastrophes, and she knew from experience how circumstances can alter your life. She had watched the illness of her stepfather deplete the family funds over a period of years. Not only did she have to face the loss of her stepfather when he died, but she also had to live through the financial strain that quickly followed. She and her mother had to uproot themselves and move to a less prosperous area just to survive. Anything that I tried to say to minimize our situation would come off as a Pollyanna answer; we both knew my wrongdoing could very well destroy us.

"We've got to do something," she said. "We have to do *something*!"

I'll never forget how tiny she felt crying in my arms. I didn't want to ever let her go; I just wanted to protect her from the mess I'd made. I was willing to do anything to remove the pain I had brought her, but there was nothing I could do. We both cried till we were spent. After a few minutes in silence, we agreed that I had to walk in truth and then face the consequences with no attempt to conceal anything.

I knew I also had to tell my parents. They already suspected some kind of trouble in my life, because I had become more distant from them over the last year. The deeper I'd sunk into illegal practices at the bank, the less comfortable I felt around them. At first I found some solace in going to their house and just sitting in the den with them, reclining in the same chair I'd lounged in while in high school. There, in that familiar safety, I could listen to my parents' warm and easy conversation and take a brief break from reality. Being with them allowed me to temporarily regain a modicum of solidarity and rightness. But when my parents began suspecting trouble in my life and asking more pointed questions about Leesa, the children, and my job, I visited them less and less. When I did visit them, I often drove away in tears.

Now I knew I had to tell them the truth. I arranged a meeting with my mother and father and my sister, Karen, and her husband,

Robin. We all met in my parents' den, where we had always had our important discussions.

After everyone was seated, I turned off the TV and said, "I want you all to know what's been going on with me."

Everyone was quiet. My parents' grave expressions were solid evidence that they already knew I was in some kind of trouble and were now anticipating an explanation.

My family allowed me to tell my entire story without interruption. I told them everything, refusing to gloss over my mistakes or hide the fact that I was facing very real consequences for my wrongdoing.

"When you began coming around here less and less, I felt that something was wrong," my father said. "I didn't know what was going on. I just felt you were being pulled into the corporate world and further away from us."

"I guess I was pursuing the wrong thing," I said.

My mom agreed. "We felt something was going on with you, but didn't want to pry. We knew you would eventually tell us what was happening when you were ready."

"Anytime you get away from the family," Dad said, "you're susceptible to what the world has to offer."

I especially felt bad for Karen. She couldn't escape publicity over my mistake any more than Leesa. She was teaching in the very middle school that she and I had both attended. Some of her colleagues were our past teachers. A few employees had been our classmates.

She cried through the whole discussion, but not because of concern for herself or her own reputation. And it wasn't for me—

she knew I was going to make it and said as much. Her real concern was for Leesa.

"Leesa is having a rough time," I admitted. "She really needs your support right now."

"What about your girls?" she asked. "How are they doing?"

At this time Lindsey was only two months shy of turning two years old. Lauren, on the other hand, was six and inquisitive about everything. "Lindsey, of course, is too young to really know what's going on," I said. "Lauren is more aware, but we're struggling to explain everything to her."

My parents offered no criticism, but neither did they encourage me to blame anyone else for my bad decisions.

Dad and Mom told me how much they loved me and said they'd help in any way they could. They offered no criticism, but neither did they encourage me to blame anyone else for my bad decisions.

"You've done wrong," my father said, "but what's important now is what you do from here."

My mother acknowledged that I needed to be practical at this point and secure a lawyer. She was concerned about me maintaining my health throughout the consequences that were obviously in my immediate future. "No matter how hard it gets," she said, "you must only speak the truth and not cover for anyone, even yourself."

I knew they were disappointed by what I had done. At the same time, I sensed that they separated their disdain for my mistakes from their deep unconditional love for their son. I was reminded that I had enjoyed this kind of acceptance and love from them my entire life.

In early March 1997, I began managing a small corner grocery store I had purchased two years prior as an investment. The store sat just across the Kentucky border in the small town of Ironton, Ohio—about ten minutes from our home. I had named it L & L Grocery after the initials of Lauren and Lindsey. I figured this small business would provide a way for me to pay our bills as I waited for the inevitable civil suit and indictment.

The store was small, with only four aisles and a deli, but the responsibilities that came with it overwhelmed me. I didn't know anything about ordering stock or pricing items or even operating the cash register. I was struck by how my indiscretion had so quickly moved me from a position as vice president of a bank to a storekeeper cutting meat for sandwiches. But I also understood that I wasn't the same person anymore. Chasing after success was no longer my priority. I now hungered to know God better and to reignite my childhood faith. Instead of thinking about what people could give me, I wanted to know how I could help them. I no longer wanted to seek only my own good—I wanted selflessness to characterize my life.

Giving freely to others was a new lifestyle for me, so I didn't know how to practice good judgment. I began giving credit to anyone who came into my store and asked. After they filled out a simple application, they could walk out with a bag of groceries. It wasn't long before word spread, and my number of patrons increased. Most people paid me back, but a few left with free food, never to be seen again.

People of every age and economic stratum passed through the store. Local businesspeople dropped in to grab a drink or snack. Young unwed mothers came for free milk for their babies. Elderly people from a nearby government-funded high-rise sometimes needed a few staples until they received their Social Security checks. The neighborhood children frequently came in for candy, and a number of people wandered in with obvious addiction problems.

This seemingly insignificant business gave me the opportunity to interact with hundreds of people. Over time I befriended a number of customers who came in regularly, sometimes lingering at my counter just to share their problems. Between customers, I read the Bible and listened to sermons on the TV across the room. I also rewrote several books from the New Testament, paraphrasing each passage in a notebook so I could understand its meaning.

It was on a bright morning in the middle of March that I first met Don. His old red Buick rumbled up onto the sidewalk beside the store to where I could just see the back end through the corner of the window. I'd heard the long, torturous creak of bad hinges and then the slam of the door. Minutes passed, but no one appeared, so I returned to reading my Bible at the counter.

When I heard the bell jingle at the entrance, I looked up to see an unkempt elderly man slowly limping into the store. Before he made it through the entryway, the door closed on him and he forced it back, ringing the bell again—even more loudly.

"Sorry for the noise," he said. He reached up and touched the bell clapper with his finger until the ringing stopped. Then he moved slowly to the counter, his body odor coming with him. He smiled at me and asked me how I was doing and if he could get a little credit—just till the first of the month.

He said he needed some lunchmeat, so I stood up to walk back toward the meat case, but hesitated so as to let him move at his slow pace. I didn't want to hurry him, so I waited for him to pass by my counter. He rocked in a painful sway as he favored his bad leg. His dirty gray hair was combed back off his face, almost touching his shoulders. I followed a few feet behind him but could still smell the sour stench of his clothes.

After getting his items, I returned to the front counter and waited. The man didn't look healthy. When he coughed and cleared his throat repeatedly, I noticed he had no teeth. He wore tinted, thick-framed glasses that looked twenty years behind the times.

When he saw my Bible, he asked, "Are you getting anything good out of that book?"

When he saw my Bible, he asked, "Are you getting anything good out of that book?"

"It's *all* good," I said.

"Jesus," he said, "is revealed from cover to cover, from Genesis to Revelation."

I wondered how he had concluded this, so I just nodded.

"May I show you?" he asked.

"Please do."

Shifting the Bible to where we both could see, he turned the pages back through the Old Testament. His hands were dirty and his nails were yellow and untrimmed. He stopped in the third chapter of Genesis and ran his finger down the page, resting it on the phrase "tree of life."

"*This* is Jesus," he said.

I examined the verse and looked up to see him smiling at my surprise.

"Why do you think the Lord placed the flaming sword at the east of the garden?" he asked.

"To keep Adam out of the garden after he sinned," I answered.

"You probably ought to read that again," he said.

I read the passage again and said, "Yes, it was to keep Adam out of the garden."

"You probably ought to read that again."

I read it more slowly. Still convinced of my interpretation, I said, "It says the Lord used the flaming sword to keep Adam out of the garden."

Again he smiled and encouraged me to read the verse one more time.

This time I read the scripture out loud. It dawned on me for the first time that the phrase "to keep the way of the tree of life" might not mean what I had always thought.

He repeated the phrase "to keep the way" and smiled. "Most people believe that God placed the flaming sword at the Garden of

Eden to keep man away, but that isn't true. It wasn't to keep people out but to show them the way in."

"What do you mean?"

"The flaming sword is the Word of God, the Good Book, the Living Book you are reading," he said. As he spoke the truths of this passage, tears welled up in his eyes and ran down his cheeks. "The flaming sword was pointing the way to the tree of life." He hesitated in an attempt to arrest his crying, and then repeated, "It points the way to the tree of life."

I didn't know what to think of this stranger. I was moved by his passion for God's Word. He seemed curiously free from all of life's material trappings; unconcerned about keeping his emotions in check, he unashamedly cried about the Lord's truths. He appeared to have nothing but a burning attraction to all that reflected Jesus. I found myself also moved to tears.

He then flipped to the twelfth chapter of Exodus where Moses tells the elders of Israel to dip the hyssop in the blood of the Passover lamb and strike the lintel and two side posts. "The blood of the lamb is the shadow of Jesus, Who is next to come," he said. "The doorpost is us."

Next he found the twenty-first chapter of Numbers where Moses made a brass serpent and raised it on a pole.

"The serpent represents Christ on the cross," he said. "Whenever the Israelites gazed upon it, they were healed." When he talked about Jesus' suffering and humiliation, he broke down and cried again.

As he turned from book to book in the Bible—all the way to

Revelation—showing me passages portraying Christ, I was amazed. I had read these same scriptures many times but had never seen what he was now pointing out. This fresh insight ignited a desire in me to reexamine everything I had ever read. I wondered what else I might have misunderstood. I wanted to digest every chapter, every verse, and every word to make sure I didn't miss anything.

He wiped his eyes and said he appreciated me giving him groceries. I watched him brace himself with one hand on the counter as he slowly filled out the credit application. Each time he coughed he raised the pen until his body stopped shaking and then continued writing in his loose, uncontrolled scrawl.

He thanked me again and said, "I'll see you later, son." Then he turned and left. I heard the loud metallic groan and slam of his car door and the repeated gunning of a dying engine. Finally his Buick backed off the sidewalk and clamored down the road.

His application mentioned only the route number of his residence. No specific address was given.

I didn't know at the time that I was going to become friends with this broken man and that we were going to spend almost every day together for the next two years. God had brought this unusual man to be my mentor. Our friendship and growth in Christ was going to initiate something that only God could have ordained, something that was going to transform not only my life but his as well.

CHAPTER

Two

Both Leesa and I had resolved to walk in truth and to face whatever consequences came our way, but it was difficult. We prayed together and talked often about trusting God and trying to know His will, but there were also many long silences. During these times, I would anguish over everything I had done to drag down my wife and children. I had sincerely returned to the Lord and was committed to living right, but that didn't suddenly rid me of the consequences following my bad decisions.

I'd watch Leesa move about the kitchen preparing a meal or

listen to her read stories to our children, providing sustenance and care as she always did, but I could tell she was suffering with the burden I had placed on her. I'd see it in her eyes when sitting at the table and hear it in her voice even when we weren't talking about our problem. And the problem was far from being over. We both knew a lawsuit or even criminal charges were coming our way. Neither of us knew where these threats would take us. Sometimes my guilt would overwhelm me, and I would succumb to tears and bury my head in my hands.

One morning I turned the chair in my office to watch Lauren play in the backyard. It was still March and too cold to swim, but she had all of her dolls sitting along the edge of our pool, ready for the approaching summer. I couldn't see Leesa from my vantage point, but I knew she was on the back porch ironing the girls' Sunday dresses. I could hear the rattle of Lindsey's baby walker moving over the porch floor as Leesa called out to Lauren.

"It's too cold to think about swimming just yet," she told her.

"When can we swim?"

"We'll just have to wait for the days to warm up, sweetheart."

Lauren looked over the pool and back to her mother. "The day seems warmer already."

Leesa laughed at her quick comment and Lauren smiled back.

"It won't be too much longer," Leesa said.

I had often heard them out back, but this time it struck me that all of this was going to end. This quiet, safe place where Leesa rocked Lindsey, read stories to the girls, or supervised a group of rowdy neighborhood children was slipping away because of me.

We likely wouldn't live in this house or have access to a pool when the days did, indeed, warm up. I was suddenly struck with panic, desperately wanting to hold on to what we had.

This quiet, safe place was slipping away because of me.

Leesa had dreamed of living in this neighborhood ever since she had lived in Ashland as a young girl. She'd thought about this area even after her family moved to the small town of Catlettsburg, a few miles away. Her mother had continued bringing her to the same school, so she had never really felt separated from her hometown. After her stepfather's death forced them to move from Catlettsburg into a duplex across the border in Ironton, Ohio, she thought often of this particular part of Ashland. She remembered the brightly painted homes with their trimmed lawns, the conversations of neighbors drifting from their porches, and the sidewalks busy with children at play.

After we married, we both worked hard with the vision of someday moving into Leesa's favorite part of Ashland. After living in Ironton, then moving to Jackson, Ohio, and back to Ironton, we finally were able to move into our dream neighborhood.

Settling in this neighborhood was better than we had ever imagined. We developed friendships with neighbors who had children close to our daughters' ages. In a very short while, we were consistently spending time with six other couples. It didn't take long for our homes to become the common playground for all of our children. We barbecued, attended ball games, and traveled to Disney World together. We couldn't imagine a better neighborhood.

Although Leesa and our girls were innocent of my illegal affairs, they still suffered the consequences. My actions had placed them directly in the line of fire. Knowing that my grocery store couldn't keep us afloat, I couldn't help but wonder just how long it would be before everything came apart and dropped us headlong into financial ruin.

If nothing else, I knew I had to keep my family in church. In the past, there had been many times when I'd told my older daughter I couldn't go with her to church because Sunday was the only day I could rest from my long hours at the bank. My reluctance to go to church began when I was a boy. The pastor of our church repeatedly spoke against children playing sports, so my participation in basketball meant I was never accepted as an integral part of the church. By the time I was fifteen, I was frequently arguing with my mother about the pastor's stand against sports; I insisted that I didn't want to go to church because I didn't fit in. She knew I had found a niche for myself through sports and eventually tired of my resistance. Finally she succumbed to my rebellion, and I stopped attending church.

I could look back and understand a fifteen-year-old boy struggling to find his way, but I hated myself as the adult who lay in bed and refused to join his family on Sunday. Now that our life was in such disarray, I was sure to be with them in church every time the doors opened.

In fact, Leesa and I were part of a core Bible group with six other couples. It was a respite for us, a place where Leesa and I felt welcome. We were completely open with our group, telling them from the beginning about what I'd done and about our unpredictable future. Thanks to their particular positions, two members, Mary and Mike, were able to help Leesa and me understand how my case could unfold. Mary was a lawyer, and Mike was an administrator with the Federal Bureau of Prisons in Summit, Kentucky, just outside of Ashland.

Leesa and I both knew that this gathering was the right place for us to be during this time. On days when Leesa was especially burdened with fear or I was drowning in guilt over my actions, we were tempted to hide in our house and not venture out to see anyone. But we both knew we needed this fellowship, so we constantly reminded each other of the dangers of isolating ourselves. We knew it was imperative that we stay involved with people who knew the truth and loved us anyway.

When I first told Leesa about Don, she didn't quite know what to make of him. But she had always had a tender place in her heart for those who seemed to be outcasts of society, and she was immediately sympathetic toward my new acquaintance.

"Where does he live?" she asked.

"I don't know."

"Do you think he sleeps in his car?"

"He might, but I don't think so."

"You would think there would be someone to take care of him."

I could tell the story deeply disturbed Leesa. Her compassion spilled out liberally for others, undiminished by our own harsh circumstances.

She asked me about his background, his knowledge of the Scriptures, and many more questions I couldn't answer. Don was still a mystery to me as well.

I hadn't been able to put down my Bible since Don had shown me the scriptures depicting Jesus. He had given me just enough of a taste to make me hungry for more. As I read the passages more slowly, I began noticing what he meant. This mysterious man who seemed to have appeared from nowhere had given me a key to drawing deeper truths out of the Bible. I had been reading and writing Bible paraphrases but had only gleaned general themes and story lines from the Scriptures. After only a few minutes with Don, I was discovering new truths.

This mysterious man who seemed to have appeared from nowhere had given me a key to drawing deeper truths out of the Bible.

A few days after first meeting Don, I again heard the rumbling of his red Buick and watched him pull into the same spot beside the store. It was several minutes before he appeared in the entryway, pushing the door open twice with two loud rings, as he had done before.

"Good morning, Don," I said as he came inside.

"Hello, son." He blushed as he came closer to my counter. "Sorry about the noise," he said, referring to the bell. "These old legs of mine just won't get me through that door fast enough." He was wearing the same dirty shirt and torn trousers he'd worn the first time I met him.

I couldn't help wondering if he knew how much he had stirred me with his teaching. I immediately began asking him questions about scriptures I had read but never understood. Over and over he showed me how the passages reflected Christ.

He laughed with delight over my enthusiasm. "It's just like the flaming sword, son, pointing the way to Jesus."

I apologized for peppering him with so many questions and began prefacing more questions with "This might be a stupid question, but . . ."

He stopped me after a few repetitions and said, "Son, the only stupid question is the one that is never asked."

"How is it that not everyone sees what you see in Scripture?" I asked. "I mean, why don't they see Christ reflected throughout the Bible?"

"Because many people approach the Living Word with preconceived notions," he said. "We need to read it as if we're reading it for the first time."

He closed his eyes and said, "Clear our minds and let us read with virgin hearts."

At first I thought this comment was directed to me, but then I realized he was praying out loud. This was something he did frequently as we became more comfortable with each other. He never interrupted me when I talked, but would stop in the middle of his answers to praise the Lord or to petition Him on my behalf. Then, without missing a beat, he'd continue his dialogue with me. I had a sense that he felt the Lord was continually in our midst.

He told me there were two kinds of people. "One kind reads the Bible, and it puts a burden on them," he said. "The other reads the Bible, and they're released from their burdens."

"Why the difference?" I asked.

"The one who is released by what he reads," he said, "sees the truth."

About that time two boys came into the store and began searching the shelf of candy.

Don pulled a stained handkerchief from his pocket, raised his glasses just enough to wipe his eyes, and smiled at them. "Sometimes it's hard to make a choice with all those flavors." He leaned down to where he was eye-to-eye with the boys and asked them what kind of day they were having.

I was struck by the rapport he had with these kids. The boys told him about the ball game they had just finished and their school and their dogs. They told him about their favorite teacher and what they dreamed of being when they got older. He laughed with them, hanging on their every word as if their stories were the best he'd ever heard.

After the boys chose their candy, he asked them if they knew Jesus loved them. He said, "You may not see Him, but Jesus is watching over you, laughing with you as you play with your friends."

The boys stopped and listened intently.

"It's like your mother leaning out the door listening and watching you play outside. Her love for you is so strong that she takes pleasure in your joys."

Both boys nodded. Don had given them a concrete glimpse of Jesus that they could understand.

After the two boys left, Don picked up where we had left off in our conversation. "Before you can be released, you have to see His truth," he said. "Seeing God's truth is more than just seeing your mistakes."

"What do you mean?" I couldn't help feeling that he was slowly turning his teaching on me.

"When you look at your sins, you're not looking at what Jesus has already done to free you from those sins," he said. "You can only look at one or the other." He smiled at me until tears filled his eyes. "Help us look unto Jesus, the author and finisher of our faith," he prayed.

I knew Don had something that I needed in my life. His disheveled appearance and his poor hygiene couldn't disguise the fact that he had an intimate understanding of Christ that kept him centered. That day I felt free to tell him all about my mistakes at the bank and what my family and I were facing.

Don listened to my entire story. He didn't offer any quick, pat answers or suggestions. This was only the second time I had met him, but I could tell he was moved by my troubles. I suddenly had a strange sense that I had known him much longer and could confide in him about anything.

I then came right out and asked if he could come to my store on a regular basis.

"Sure, son," he said.

I gave him gas money, but at first he didn't want to take it.

"Please," I said. "It's important for me to see you every day."

I still didn't know much about this mysterious man. Who was he? Where did he live? Had he come to me from another realm? I didn't have immediate answers, but I did know that his presence and his words brought a peace and hope into my life that I desperately needed. And I thanked God for him.

Don kept his promise. He came by my store every morning. And, of course, I always heard the loud rumble of his old red Buick before I saw him pull up to his favorite place on the walkway in front. I got used to waiting patiently for him to enter the store, minutes after I heard the creak and slam of his door.

Though he was unassuming and unimpressive by the world's standards, Don's regular presence brought me immeasurable comfort. I placed a chair for him in front of the ice cream freezer near the counter where I sat. He liked this spot because he enjoyed picking out the ice cream bars and Popsicles for the children too small to reach inside the freezer. He surprised each child by remembering his or her favorite treat.

Now and then he would hold up a different ice cream and ask, "Have you ever tasted one of these?" If the young buyer tried it, Don would laugh until his eyes teared up.

It was clear that he enjoyed the children's innocent pleasures.

At first some of the kids were a little wary of him because of his appearance, but that never lasted long. Once he engaged them in conversation and they sensed his compassionate heart, they were mesmerized by him.

At first some of the kids were a little wary of him because of his appearance, but that never lasted long.

In addition to children, the elderly and the poor gravitated toward Don. It made sense that my destitute customers had rapport with him because they knew each other outside the store, but I was curious about the relationship he had with the senior citizens, especially the obviously wealthy ones, until Don explained.

"The older ones," he said, "are from a different period. They grew up with politeness and respecting each other."

But there was one eighty-year-old man named Benedict who didn't connect with Don. He came into my store every four days for a pound of bologna and a bottle of Robitussin. No matter what kind of weather, he always wore dark sunglasses, a heavy jacket, and a continual scowl. Despite his age, he was spry enough to walk the few blocks to the store. Whenever I saw him coming, I'd go back to the meat counter to cut his bologna. Don would disappear down an aisle as quickly as he could manage.

Benedict was never rude to Don. He just appeared cantankerous and in a hurry. Don, I figured, feared some sort of criticism from him.

I soon found out, however, that there were many people who

blatantly treated Don as subservient. Some whom Don greeted only nodded and walked past him. There were even a few who looked away with no response at all.

One morning a man dressed in a suit completely ignored Don's warm "hello" and spoke only to me.

"How can I help you?" I asked.

"I've driven a bit off course," he said. "What's the quickest way to cross over into Kentucky?"

I directed him a few blocks down to the bridge. "It takes a few turns," I said. "When you pass the paint store, you'll know you're heading in the right direction."

"I shouldn't be able to miss that." He laid a pack of gum on the counter and took out his wallet. A loose twenty-dollar bill fell on the floor.

Don leaned forward from his chair at the ice cream freezer and knelt down to retrieve the man's money. Just before he reached it, the stranger quickly pressed his foot onto the bill. Don stopped for a moment in surprise, then slowly moved back to his seat as the man picked up his money.

Don sat still, looking down to the floor. After the man left the store he looked up, his eyes wet with tears, and said, "He must not have seen me."

WHEN I FINALLY TOLD my Bible study group about Don, I could tell that some were skeptical. The more I explained his appearance and his understanding of the Scriptures, the more far-fetched my tale seemed. It wasn't difficult for them to believe that an impoverished man would regularly come to my store and chat. What they couldn't reconcile was my description of Don's appearance and his wisdom concerning the scriptures—the Living Word, as Don always said.

"I mean, is this man a retired pastor down on his luck?" Bill asked. "I don't see how somebody can have all that knowledge of the Bible and basically just live on the street."

"Could he just be parroting what he's heard from another preacher?" Mary asked.

I couldn't satisfactorily answer any of their questions. Don was as much of an enigma to me as he was to them.

"Have you ever seen where he goes after he visits you?" Mary's husband, Tim, asked.

"No," I said.

"Well, do you have any idea where he lives?" asked Bill.

"No, I don't. I've never pushed the point with him."

"Have you seen him talk with anybody else besides you?"

"I've seen him talk with the kids who come into my store for candy," I said. "Why?"

"Bill is wondering if Don could be an angel," Mary said.

"Bill is wondering if Don could be an angel," Mary said.

Mike and his wife looked at me for some kind of response.

There was a sudden silence among the group, and then a slight chuckle.

Bill threw up his arms and said, "I don't hear any other solution from anyone else that makes sense."

"Why don't you follow him sometime?" Tim asked. "At least try to find out where he lives."

When Leesa and I drove home that night, I told her that the whole debate over Don was almost humorous. "It's easier for them to believe me about all my wrongdoings at the bank than to believe me about Don."

"I think they believe you," she said. "They're just groping for more information about him. He's such a mystery."

I knew she was right.

I couldn't really blame anyone who was suspicious of my story. When I was away from the store and thinking about this stranger who had suddenly come into my life, even I could hardly believe it.

LATER THAT WEEK Mike and Bill surprised me with a visit at the store. They came in to see me occasionally, but it was unusual for them to come together. They had arrived at the best time to get a glimpse of Don, who was sitting beside the counter.

"What brings you two out today?" I asked, knowing that they wanted to get a closer look at my new friend.

"We were out this way and wanted to drop in on you," Mike said, glancing over at Don.

I introduced everyone, explaining to Don about my connection with them in a Bible study group.

Bill smiled and said, "It's a pleasure to meet you."

I could see the strain in Don's face as he stood up.

I tried drawing him into the conversation, but he said he had better look for a few items before heading home, and then walked slowly down an aisle.

The three of us continued talking among ourselves, but it was merely insignificant chitchat. Our attention was drawn toward Don, who was now completely out of sight. I could see the wonder in their eyes. I knew they too had picked up on his discomfort at meeting them. I was really struck by his response because he talked so freely with me and with the children who came into the store. I didn't know if he felt he was intruding on our conversation or if he was just ill at ease around other adults. Mike and Bill weren't offensive or intimidating in any way, as far as I could see.

I don't even remember how my friends' visit ended or what they said when they departed because I was so focused on Don. After they left, Don appeared with a couple cans of vegetables. He was unusually quiet as he paid. Then he left.

I thought about Don's reaction to my friends and about everybody's questions in my last Bible study meeting. Then I remembered that Don had filled out his credit application without including a specific address, only listing the route number.

I decided to leave an hour early the next morning and see if I could locate Don's house. I figured I would drive up and down his road and search for his red Buick.

His road was narrow and led deep into a hollow filled with shanties. The homes were either faded mobile homes or tiny, weathered frame houses long overdue for paint and repair. Some places had broken windows and sagging roofs. A few had porches, usually cluttered with discarded furniture. Most of the tiny yards were littered with old tires and debris.

I drove slowly, glancing between homes and inside open garages for his car, but found nothing.

At first I was surprised by the number of people apparently living on this stretch of road, judging by the number of cars parked alongside or in front of the homes. Then I realized that many of the vehicles were broken down, long ago abandoned.

At one point I got a glimpse of red that I was sure had to be Don's old Buick on the far side of a clapboard shack. But when I came closer, I realized it wasn't his car but a dilapidated plaid couch, apparently thrown out as trash.

Eventually the surface of the country lane became marred with potholes and collapsed shoulders around the curves. I drove until the road ended at the foot of a small abandoned house nestled on a hill, still not finding Don's car.

I parked and stepped out to scan the length of the neighborhood. The hills rose high on both sides, enclosing the entire hollow in a suffocating, damp stench.

It was the first time I had seriously considered the plight of the poor. I wondered about the story of each person in every one of the shacks, what had brought them or their parents to live here. I had never really feared ending up in poverty like this until my indiscretion at the bank. The very real possibility of dragging my family from our home to this kind of place was too much for me to face.

I decided to end my search for Don. I got into my car and drove to work.

When Don came into the store that day, I asked him where he lived. "I was out on your road but never saw your Buick."

His countenance dropped. I could see he was embarrassed.

"I'll tell you, son," he said. "It may not be the kind of place you'd expect."

He hesitated as if he didn't really want to explain, and I didn't know what to say.

"It's just a small shack without any water or heat, but I have a phone so I can call my children," he said. "Not much of a home, but the owner is kind enough to let me live there."

I knew then I should never ask him about it again.

CHAPTER
Three

ON A SATURDAY MORNING in the first week of April, I saw my face on the front page of the newspaper before I had even opened the paper dispenser. The photo had been taken just a few months earlier at the newspaper office to publicize my recent promotion to vice president. When I read the article, I had the awful feeling of finally meeting up with the catastrophe I knew was coming. The article named only me in a civil lawsuit. My former partners in the land development business had separated themselves from me and obtained their own lawyers. The article was not accurate, claiming that I had taken money from all their bank accounts.

The photo that had originally represented success and a bright direction for my career was now a humiliating portrayal of how far I had fallen. The public exposure was far-reaching in our small town of thirteen thousand people. The newspaper office where the photo had been taken was less than a mile from my corner store. And the paper itself had a large readership.

I was devastated. I had expected consequences for my sins, but I'd never imagined I'd be front-page news. I was horrified at the thought of how all of this was going to affect my family.

I went back to my car and called Leesa.

"How did you ever get us into this trouble?" she asked.

"I'm sorry, Lee."

"What are we going to do?" she asked. I could hear the fear in her voice.

"I don't know," I said.

"You can disappear into your store, but I have to face everyone at work."

Her words cut deep. What she said couldn't have been more true. Her concerns, however, weren't about her boss. She worked for Dr. Triplett-Schweickart, a very kind podiatrist who cared about Leesa and encouraged her whenever she was down. Instead, Leesa was troubled about the many people she saw as she worked at the doctor's two locations. Between the Ironton office and the office across from Bellefonte Hospital in Ashland, she saw a number of doctors, staff, and patients who would know everything that was going on. I was sure Dr. Triplett-Schweickart, well known and much involved in the community, was privy to a lot of disparaging comments that she tactfully kept from Leesa.

Over the past three months, as more time had passed since my resignation, we had begun speculating about whether the bank would sue me. But now, with the publicized civil lawsuit, we had to face the likelihood of a court case. Our present conversation was as upsetting as when I had first told Leesa about my wrongdoing at the bank.

"We're going to lose our home," she said. "What are we going to do then?"

"I'll think of something," I said, not knowing what else to say.

"Being forced out of your home is humiliating," she said. "After my stepfather died, I just kept thinking there had to be some way Mother and I could keep our house, but there wasn't. I thought of every possible way we could stay, but there was no answer."

"We're going to lose our home," she said. "What are we going to do then?"

"I know, Lee. I know it was hard for you back then."

"No, you don't know until you go through it," she said. "It wasn't just a matter of my mother and me leaving a nice home." She broke into tears. "It was the whole upheaval of our lives."

"I'm sorry, Lee."

"As far as I'm concerned, I could live anywhere," she said. "I'm more upset over how this is changing the future for our girls. We both worked hard to provide for them. Now it looks like we're going to lose everything."

I couldn't think of what else to say to Leesa. I felt myself sinking into a paralyzing fear of what was to become of her and my two daughters. I hated myself more than ever for dragging them into this.

"Aren't you going to say something?" she asked.

"I know you want something tangible to fix everything, but I can't give it to you, Lee. I'd give up my life if it could preserve you and our girls. I don't know what to do any more than you do."

After we ended the call, I immediately called Don and asked him to come to my store before it opened.

He didn't ask the reason. He said, "I'll be there right away, son," and hung up.

The most comforting sound I heard that morning was the rumble and rattle of Don's old red Buick pulling up alongside the store. After the familiar creak and slam of his door, he finally appeared and moved to his chair by the counter.

"What's wrong, son?"

I started to explain, but got choked up and just handed him the newspaper.

I was hoping Don would show me a passage out of the Scriptures that would reveal some strategy of escape from all the mess I had created. But Don didn't reach for the Bible. Instead, he stood and rested his hands on my shoulders and began to pray aloud. He asked the Lord to let me see everything with His eyes.

"Through this journey, precious Jesus," he said, "secure the love and marriage of Kevin and Leesa that you have sealed in heaven."

He and I prayed and cried together. Then Don listened quietly as I told him about my talk with Leesa and how our marriage was disintegrating.

"I can't even promise her that I'll be here a month from now to provide for her and our children," I said. "I have made an endless number of wrong decisions, and now we are in a corner."

"I know, son," Don said. "But you must understand that the way to overcome a series of bad decisions is by making a series of good decisions."

"The way to overcome a series of bad decisions is by making a series of good decisions."

"But how? It seems too late. I feel we're at the end of the line."

Don prayed aloud again and then said to me, "'A man's heart deviseth his way: but the Lord directeth his steps.'" I didn't answer, and he added, "That scripture is for you too, no matter what mistakes you've made."

"I don't know how we're going to survive this," I said.

"That's up to you, son. It's your choice. You can allow this problem to destroy you and take you down, or you can use it to strengthen you and take you up. And depending on your decision, this will either pull you and Leesa together or ruin you." He paused and stared at me for a moment. "One more suggestion."

"What's that?"

"Don't say anything to your accusers. Let God speak."

I didn't know exactly what he meant by this, but I knew my natural inclination was to give answers and aggressively defend myself.

"What about people I know who want to know the truth?"

"You must always speak the truth, but don't fall into a position of defense," he said. "That's exactly when you'll become entangled."

I meant to follow his advice, but the very next day I read an article in another paper that had even more incorrect details about the lawsuit against me. Some of the information was correct, but some of it was blatantly wrong. I fully expected that I would be exposed publicly after the first article came out, but I wanted the newspapers to be accurate. I sat for a while fuming at how the false details about my indiscretion were giving it an increasingly sinister tone. I was especially worried about Leesa reading it.

I called the editor's office and tried to clarify some of the facts. The more I talked, the more I could feel it wasn't the right thing to do. I was lowering myself to a position of defense, just as Don had warned against. After I hung up the phone, I knew not to do this again. I realized I wasn't clarifying anything but just stoking the fires of growing rumor and innuendo.

Most of the clientele frequenting my store never recognized me as the vice president named in the lawsuit. I was almost separated and hidden, handing out groceries to some customers who probably couldn't even afford the luxury of subscribing to the newspaper that first exposed me. This anonymity, coupled with the comfort of seeing Don every day, made my corner grocery a respite and safeguard.

Leesa didn't have the same protection, especially after accepting a new job as a teacher's assistant at Oakview Elementary. She was involved not only with her students but with their parents as well. She had periodic meetings with her principal and colleagues and was also involved in Lauren's school activities. She was constantly under the scrutiny of people who knew about me, a few of whom were indiscreet with their pointed comments.

One afternoon I called Leesa as she was driving home from school. I could tell she was upset, even though she was doing her best not to display it to Lauren, Lindsey, and the neighborhood children she taxied back and forth every day.

"What's going on?" I asked.

"I'm just getting weary of the constant attention over the situation."

The situation was the way we referred to our problem whenever we spoke in front of the girls.

"Another friend avoiding me in the cafeteria," she said, "and another well-meaning comment."

When she got home and we were alone, she told me how a colleague had walked into the cafeteria, seen her, and quickly turned to exit down the hallway. The well-meaning comment from a longtime acquaintance was, "We don't believe any of these vicious lies about your husband. And we want you to know that we're praying for both of you."

Even encouraging comments from the sincerest of friends were upsetting, because Leesa was caught in the middle. If she tried to clarify the true details about my sin, more questions would be asked and she would soon be placed in the exhausting position of defending herself. This was exactly what Don had warned me about. On the other hand, saying little or nothing kept her defenseless amidst exaggeration and rumors.

One Saturday afternoon, Leesa quickly returned home after leaving to go shopping with our two daughters.

"Why are you back so soon?" I asked. It was the expression on her face rather than the lack of groceries that told me something terrible had happened.

After Leesa sent the girls back to play in their bedroom, she said, "I can never escape people talking about the lawsuit."

"What happened?"

"I was halfway through my shopping," she said. "I heard two people in the next aisle talking about you."

"What did they say?"

"They said they couldn't believe how you stole all that money from the bank."

"Who were they?" I felt like my whole insides were pushing up into my chest.

"I don't know, and it really doesn't matter," she said. "There's no escaping this."

"What did you do?"

"There's absolutely no escaping from all this," she repeated, as if she hadn't heard my question.

"Lee, what did you do?"

"I had a basket full of groceries," she said. "I picked up Lindsey out of her seat, took Lauren by her hand, and walked out of the store. I just left the basket in the middle of the aisle."

Not long after the news article about the lawsuit came out, some of the close friends in our neighborhood began dropping out of our lives. Many of the relationships we had built over time vanished in the face of my mistakes. This was difficult for Leesa and for me. It hurt as much as if members of our own family had abandoned us.

The hardest part was trying to explain to Lauren. While we were blessed with some wonderful neighbors who supported us and never discussed our predicament with their children, there were others who no longer allowed their kids to play with Lauren. All she knew was that some of her neighborhood friends were no longer coming around.

"Why won't Sarah ride bikes with me anymore?" she asked one Saturday morning. Our once-busy front sidewalk was now empty. Her friends no longer came and called out for her. Now the sound of children playing came only from several houses away. "And where's Hannah? She never comes to play."

"Their family wanted to go in a different direction in life," I told her.

"But we were all good friends," she said.

"You're still good friends," Leesa told her. "Sometimes families just become involved with other things."

When Leesa knelt down and held her, Lauren cried. "If they're my friends," she said, "they should play down here."

It was at times like these that I saw clearly how my actions had harmed the most vulnerable ones in my family. It got to where the laughing and frivolity of children down the street made me want to bring Lauren inside the house and out of hearing distance. Every time she heard them, she was reminded that she was now on the outside, and she could not understand why.

Every time Lauren heard children playing down the street, she was reminded that she was now on the outside, and she could not understand why.

I COMPLETELY UNDERSTOOD why Leesa sometimes wanted to quit work and escape, but leaving her job was out of the question. She and I both knew that I could very well be going to prison. Then she and our girls would have to survive somehow on her income. Sometimes she also wanted to quit our Bible study group and stop going to church to avoid seeing people, but we continued.

Knowing that Leesa was facing the consequences of my wrong choices made me loathe myself more every day. Each time she told me about someone gossiping against us or about old friends avoiding her, I felt less and less worthy to have ever married this good woman. She and I were both sincere about facing the truth—as we'd agreed back in January—but this didn't make the day-to-day struggle any easier. Our time together was spent either talking about our problem or enduring evenings and weekends in depressing silence. Without any warning, Leesa would break down and cry. Other times we found ourselves arguing over the most mundane problems: a broken glass at dinner, misplaced keys, or my trousers carelessly left draped over a chair.

Three weeks after the appearance of the first news article, I began to think I could no longer bear living with her. It had gotten to where I didn't want to come home after work each day. My problem was that I hated myself, and I hated what I imagined she thought when she looked at me. I knew I was letting our predicament divide us—as Don had cautioned against—but I was physically and emotionally spent, without any possible solution for my family.

I wanted to be near my father. He was always the calming force in our family. No matter the circumstances, nothing ever seemed to rattle him. Years ago, when the Coca-Cola bottling plant sold out, he lost his position as manager, but he never fretted. My mother inquired for jobs through all her contacts while Dad searched and submitted an endless number of résumés. Both worked diligently, but neither one panicked, especially my father.

Throughout this lengthy search, my mother always honored him and consistently said, "God's going to come through."

The problem was finding a decent job in an economically depressed area, but Dad finally obtained a position as a garbage collector. I was fourteen years old with a strong sense of my image as a jock, so I couldn't understand my father's humility in accepting a much lower position than he'd had. Even more surprising to me was that my mother and father both thanked the Lord for his new job. When I saw how he happily traded in his business suit for jeans and work boots to ride on the back of a garbage truck, it made it easier for me to accept. I knew not to worry about his disgrace, because he wasn't humiliated. Working was honorable and he was providing for his family. I began to realize that my father never made a distinction between people. Whether he worked for top management of a large company or was under the authority of the driver of a sanitation truck, he respected his boss and did his best. When he had the opportunity later to drive the truck, he chose to continue riding on the back until he retired.

One evening during dinner with Leesa and my girls, I made the decision to leave. It wasn't because of an argument with Leesa, but because of my own selfishness. I didn't want to watch the pain I had caused. Watching my wife and two girls was like looking into a mirror that reflected my wrong actions. Whenever Leesa cried about someone's careless remark at work or whenever she asked me about upcoming bills or the unpredictability of our future, I knew I was facing myself and what I had done to my family.

After our girls left the table to play, Leesa asked me what we were going to do about our troubles. It was the same question she had asked over and over, and rightfully so, but I couldn't give her an answer. It wasn't that she and I had an intense confrontation. It was simply the same emotional strain that was always with us. But now I couldn't take it anymore.

"Lee, I don't know what we're going to do," I said. "I tell you, I just need to . . ." Without finishing my sentence, I left the table and went to our bedroom. I pulled out a suitcase and began packing my clothes.

"What are you doing?" Leesa asked from the doorway.

I pulled out a suitcase and began packing my clothes.

I didn't answer.

"Where are you going?"

"Lee, I just need some space, and you do too. I struggle with the guilt, and I hate myself for all I've done to you and the girls. I think of this every hour of the day."

"Are you really leaving us?"

"No," I said, looking back at her. "I just need to stay at my parents' awhile until everything settles and I can figure out what to do."

"You can't leave us."

"I'm not leaving you. I'm still taking care of you. I just can't endure seeing how I'm dragging you down."

"We love each other," she said.

"Of course we love each other."

"Are you going to let the Enemy do this to us?" she asked.

I shut my suitcase and sat on the edge of the bed. Don's words resounded in my ears. He had told me that it was my choice whether this situation destroyed our marriage or made us stronger. "No," I said, "I'm not going to let anything tear us apart."

Leesa sat beside me on the bed, and we cried together. We promised each other that we were going to actively choose to let our troubles make us stronger. We vowed then never to talk about separation or divorce.

I looked up to see our two girls standing at the door, watching and crying also.

"Everything is all right, girls," I said. "Your mother and I are just getting ready to pray together."

Leesa held out her hand to them and said, "Why don't you come and pray with Mommy and Daddy?"

We all huddled together. Leesa and I held our girls as they folded their tiny hands in prayer. Then we thanked the Lord for each other and our babies. I asked God to forgive my self-centeredness and my fears. I also asked the Lord to help me see His face and not just my mistakes.

EVERY MORNING Don came into my store carrying a discarded gum wrapper or the paper stick from a sucker he'd picked up from my parking lot.

"Some child must have been in a real hurry to get to this piece of candy," he'd say, holding it out for me to see. Sometimes he'd flatten out the foil from a candy bar that had been balled up and joyfully examine it.

At first I thought he was simply eccentric, but slowly I began to see that he received pleasure in ways that others didn't. His love for children fueled his imagination to the point where he could see the world from their perspective and understand their simple joys.

That's why he could gaze upon the wrinkled wrapper and laugh at the thought of a child hurriedly throwing it aside to devour the candy.

After I realized he loved buttermilk, I made sure to always keep it in stock at the store. He'd drink it straight from the carton, smack his lips, and say, "Buttermilk is good for you, just like the milk and honey written in God's Word."

At first I thought he was simply eccentric, but slowly I began to see that he received pleasure in ways that others didn't.

After a while of giving Don snacks and lunches, I eventually convinced him to let me take him out to eat. This was a big step in our relationship because he had resisted ever since we had met. He always politely declined and quietly withdrew, as he did when well-dressed customers came into the store. I wondered if he just didn't want to be out in public with me. I feared he thought his appearance would embarrass me, especially when he ate. Since he didn't have any teeth, he had to gum his food, working his lower jaw back and forth until it became mush. This was often a lengthy and messy ordeal.

I let Don choose the place, and we ended up at a local hamburger shop. When he spoke to several street people sipping coffee in groups at different tables, I knew he had been here many times before. I could tell he had close ties with each of them.

"How come they're not eating lunch?" I asked after we sat down.

"They can't afford it."

"Of course," I said. "I should have known better." It dawned on me just how far removed I was from Don's world.

"It's okay, son," he said. He pointed at a man about fifty years old wearing a blue bandana. He was sitting at a table alone, staring out the window. "That man lost everything."

"What happened?"

"His child was killed, and it destroyed him and his marriage."

"Was it his fault?"

"No."

"Then why did he allow it to—"

"It doesn't have to be your fault for something to rupture your life."

"It doesn't have to be your fault for something to rupture your life," he said before I finished my question. He nodded his head at his friends. "Not everybody got here because of their bad decisions. Sometimes it's because of other people's bad decisions."

I couldn't help wondering what Don's story was, how a man with such wisdom and love for God's Word could end up as he had.

Don talked with such intensity that he was oblivious to the coffee dripping into his beard and the grease from his sandwich running down his arm. "You need to see this, son. Everyone is valuable. Everybody is someone's daughter or son or father or mother. There is treasure in every life if you choose to see it."

He cried with his last words and pressed his hands over his mouth.

I figured then that Don had purposely brought me to this restaurant where he knew he could teach me. After he calmed himself, he said, "The man in the blue bandana is even educated. He just never got past his loss."

"Why couldn't he?"

"Self-inflicted guilt is as damaging as true guilt," he said. "No one can experience the abundant life Jesus promised by hating what they were before they were saved. They have to understand who they are now in the eyes of the Lord."

I knew then that he was talking about me.

CHAPTER

Four

ONE DAY IN OUR DISCUSSIONS, I discovered that Don had once attended the very church I had abandoned when I was fifteen years old. There was a different pastor back then, but he was there during the period when my mother was a young member and my grandfather was an elder. During our talks about the church, I tried to find out whether he had some kind of relationship with anyone I might have known. Just to satisfy my curiosity, I wanted to see if he had any connections with real family or long-standing friends from his past.

Occasionally he would mention a daughter who lived in Columbus.

"Fruit never falls far from its tree," I said to him one time when he mentioned her visiting. "I bet she's a lot like you."

"I guess she just might be," he said with a laugh.

"I'd like to meet her."

"Well, she just came and left last week," he answered.

"When's the next time she'll be coming in?"

"It's hard to say. She's so busy coming and going."

I soon realized he never mentioned seeing his daughter until she was already heading back toward Columbus. This, of course, ensured that I could never meet her. Soon I began doubting that he even had a daughter or any family at all. His continual dodging of my questions made him an even greater mystery to me. He was such a dichotomy of brokenness and spiritual wisdom that I still did not understand this man, even after knowing him for six months. The longer I went without proof of him having family, the more I reflected on the scripture in Hebrews that talked about people entertaining angels without knowing it.

The longer I knew him, the more I reflected on the scripture in Hebrews about people entertaining angels without knowing it.

One afternoon I gave credit to a middle-aged customer named Leon who still owed me money for the last two months. He had the practice of always promising to pay next week, but only returned for more free items. Don waited until the man was out of the store with his two bags of groceries before he said, "There's a big difference between living in the wilderness and living in the promised land."

"Yes?" I said.

"My son, the Lord never means for us to be a doormat."

"You mean I shouldn't keep giving credit to people like Leon."

"Listen, son, you need to come out of that wilderness thinking." Don chuckled to soften his direct comment, as was his habit. "As a child of God in the promised land, you can't let people keep walking on you. You are to be more assertive."

"I've tried so hard to stop being selfish that I've become imprudent," I said, "but why are we to be more assertive?"

"While you're in the wilderness, you're waiting for something to happen. You're not creating anything because you have an entitlement attitude. You don't have to produce the manna; you just wait for it to appear."

"I never thought about it quite like that before."

"Here in the promised land you can't be lazy; you have to create your own manna. In the wilderness you're afraid and just holding on to what you have." He pointed to his dilapidated brown shoe, the shoelace too short to reach the last eyelets because of previous breaks, and smiled. "You know what I'm talking about—the wilderness where shoes don't wear out."

I laughed with him, enjoying his unique way to poke fun.

"You can ask Ray Wilson about it because he was in the Living Manna Trio at your old church," he said. "They sang about this."

"How do you know about that group?" I asked, trying as I had before to draw out any information that connected him to my previous church. "Do you have their albums?"

"No," he said. "I just remember hearing them sing at church."

"Did you know Ray Wilson or talk to him much?"

"No, I never talked too much with Ray."

At this point I could tell Don was slowly shifting away from my inquiries, and I just couldn't press him any further.

I had asked my mother if she'd known Don when he attended their church, but she didn't remember him. This didn't really surprise me because she was only in her teens then and was mostly involved with people her age. But she did remember seeing him years later—an elderly poor man on the streets of Ironton. I also learned that my dad knew of Don. During that period he was still collecting trash, and he often saw Don moving about in different parts of the town. He never knew much about him. Neither did my cousin Randy, who also picked up garbage at that time but in a different section of the city. Don was a mystery to everyone I asked.

Driven by my growing curiosity, I became more aggressive in searching for answers. I asked my mother to ask questions about Don next time she saw Ray Wilson or any older church members. I enlisted my father and cousin Randy to be on the lookout to see if Don ever interacted with anyone besides his usual friends living on the streets. I even began calling friends I remembered from my old church, asking them to inquire about Don with their parents or grandparents. I sat at my store counter making one call after another during the part of the day when I knew Don wouldn't be there. Like an amateur detective, I secretly jotted down every name or church event Don mentioned.

Part of me felt uneasy pursuing this information behind Don's back. I well remembered how he'd responded when he discovered I was searching for his home. However, I just couldn't put aside the mystery surrounding this man. How could someone be so downtrodden and separated from mainstream society, and yet exude such an eternal wisdom?

How could someone be so downtrodden and separated from mainstream society, and yet exude such an eternal wisdom?

In the end, I came up with nothing. There were people who remembered seeing this impoverished, timid man, but nothing else. In fact, I knew more about him than any of my contacts.

One day I asked Don if he remembered my grandfather.

"No, son, I don't remember him," he said.

I described him and added, "He was an elder during the time you were at the church."

"Well, son, that was quite a few years back."

My own memory of my grandfather was limited because he died when I was five years old. My most vivid recollection of him involved an incident that strangely hinted at the period when I would meet Don.

My grandfather worked at an iron plant in Ironton, but also owned a corner grocery just a block from where I grew up. Mom would take me to the store on days when he was managing it. I always enjoyed seeing my grandfather, but sometimes resisted going if I didn't feel like walking the distance. To keep me entertained and at a steady pace, Mom would let me ride my toy red car for these trips. This special ride offered an extra enticement to accompany my mother.

Mom would say, "Let's go ride your car to see Paw Paw." In a matter of minutes I'd be beside her pushing with my feet and coasting over the dips and cracks of the sidewalk leading directly to the store.

During one visit, Paw Paw presented me with a laminated driver's license that he had created with paper and markers. Even though I knew him as a sweet man with a good sense of humor, I also knew his serious side. He always spoke with authority about being responsible and always choosing to do right. When he presented me with the license, I sensed his approval and was motivated to continue making those trips in my car. I felt that I now had a legal document that empowered me with special rights.

After that, when my mother said, "Let's go ride your car to see Paw Paw," I felt a deeper connection with my grandfather and that I was traveling for some special purpose.

A boy empowered by a license he carried as he drove his red car to the corner grocery was strangely similar to Don delivering the authority of Scripture to my store in his rusty red Buick. Some might say it was prophetic, but I didn't really know how to view it. However, I did know that it uniquely reflected what was yet to come.

Whenever I reflect on being empowered by the Lord to fulfill

His mission, my mind always comes back to the time I received that unusual gift from my grandfather.

One morning I saw my elderly customer, Benedict, marching toward the store in his dark sunglasses, his heavy jacket, and his usual angry expression.

"Here he comes," I said, giving Don the chance to hide down one of the aisles. "I better start cutting his bologna."

Benedict picked up his Robitussin and stood at the meat counter. "One pound of bologna," he said as if I hadn't heard this same request a hundred times over.

After Benedict left and was far out of sight, Don returned to his chair near my counter. A few minutes later a woman came in whom I remembered as a devout member from my old church. She still refused to wear makeup or cut the long hair that reached past the middle of her back. The hem of her dress rose only a few inches above her shoes.

I could tell by her expression that she recognized Don. She tried to turn down an aisle out of sight, but Don smiled and called her by name. She returned the greeting and continued walking.

After the woman bought some items and left, Don asked me if I knew her.

"Yes, I remember her from our old church."

"She was there when I was there too," he said. "I know both her and her mother."

"I never knew her mother," I said.

"Did you know that the women at the church never cut their hair but singe it off with a lighter because of their interpretation of Corinthians?"

"My mother told me about that," I said. "I guess that woman must still be attending our old church."

"No, she's not," Don said. "Both she and her mother have fallen away from the church."

"You sure couldn't tell it by looking at her."

"That's right," Don said. "From her appearance, it looks like nothing has changed."

"Why continue dressing like that if she's left the church?"

"Because she's still living under the pressure of their external standards."

"That's really amazing."

"Not so amazing when you consider that most people suffer this way," Don said. "They're struggling to project an image of what they think others want of them."

"Most people are struggling to project an image of what they think others want of them."

"Sometimes it's not just what they think others want," I added. "Often people are demanding those standards." I thought about how our old church's stance against sports had driven me away. The pastor also wouldn't baptize my sister at age twelve because she wore pants.

"That's right, son." Don sat quietly for a moment and then

added, "But we have to be sympathetic to the suffering of the oppressors; they too are acting by standards they put on themselves."

"So what's the outcome of all this?"

"If they're not looking to Christ and don't understand His complete acceptance, they may appear on top of the world but remain empty inside. The reason is that they are believing a lie."

We were interrupted by the bell at the front door, and I turned to see Chris, a friend from church, walk in. When he came up to the counter, I introduced him to Don.

Don stood up and spoke, but he looked uncomfortable, just as he had with Mike and Bill.

Chris smiled at Don. "Kevin has it too good. He can pretend he's working while enjoying the company of a good friend."

"There's not a better friend than Don," I said.

Don smiled faintly but didn't answer.

"Where do you live, Don?" my friend asked.

It was a casual question just to make light conversation, but more stress registered in Don's face. "Here all my life, haven't I, Kevin?"

After I answered yes, Don excused himself and disappeared down one of the aisles.

When Chris left, Don came back to his chair. I didn't ask him about his peculiar response, as I never did. As I got to know Don, I consciously made the effort never to embarrass him. Sometimes I was successful, and sometimes I was not.

My friend had only been gone for a few minutes when Don said, "Son, I know the emptiness of believing another person's lie."

With this brief acknowledgment, Don finally began telling me his story.

About forty-five years earlier, Don and his younger brother, Paul, had trained for the National Guard at Camp Grayling in Crawford County, Michigan. Don was much different during this period of his life. He said he was colder. His feelings toward people were much less compassionate. One night he was unable to sleep and just lay on his cot for hours listening to the occasional shifting and snoring of all the men in the barracks. He was haunted by his inability to get past himself to find any kind of peace. He desperately wanted relief from his growing discontent, which consumed him.

In the dark room, he sobbed to himself and whispered, "I need You, Lord; I need You and the peace You promise."

A soft light appeared several feet from his cot. At first he thought the sergeant was checking the barracks with a flashlight, but then realized there was no logical source for it. The light grew brighter and came closer like a fog until he was completely enveloped. Don wasn't afraid because he knew it was the presence of the Lord Jesus.

Don's thoughts were overpowered with the words, "You will only find peace in Me."

Because of Don's brokenness, he was able to receive the Lord into his heart. Immediately the gnawing discontent that had taunted him for many years was vanquished by a divine, overwhelming peace. Don compared it to flipping on a light in a dark room. "God separated light and darkness at the beginning of creation," he said. "When light enters a place, darkness must flee."

The experience completely changed Don. In the days that followed, he realized that he now felt a deep appreciation and love for people, even strangers he'd see from a distance. He was also overtaken with the wonder and joys of the simplest of things. He began reading the Good Book, meditating on all of God's Words, turning them over and over in his mind. Don loved church and listened closely to every sermon and conversation that expounded upon Jesus.

At first his brother, Paul, didn't quite believe the story of his encounter with Christ, but the change in Don ultimately convinced him.

After his training, Don struggled through some harsh years of seeking employment and working where he could. During this period, he was married and over time became the father of eleven children. He worked in a bakery and dug plots at a cemetery. He drove a dairy truck and delivered milk with his brother, a job he liked, but one day he struck a piece of metal lying in the road and ruptured the gas tank. He was immediately fired. His best job was with the C&O Railway, but at that point, his diabetes worsened and affected his ability to function. Nevertheless, he continued with the C&O and pressed on to support his wife and children. However, he was severely injured in a work accident, and while trying to work out disability benefits, he got into an argument with his supervisor and was fired.

"The worst part of all this," he said, "was that I always felt my wife never forgave me for losing this job." As he cried, he lifted his glasses to wipe his eyes with his handkerchief. "How can I blame her? I wish I could have done better for my beloved and all my children."

After losing his position at the railroad, he got a job driving a taxi. One evening an acquaintance approaching from the opposite direction swerved across the line and collided with his cab. Don was severely injured and hospitalized, but he recovered. The other man was killed.

Don began suffering from deep guilt and depression. He quickly spiraled downward. He was eventually hospitalized, only able to see his family on weekends.

"Then when my wife divorced me, I was completely devastated," Don said. "I couldn't bear living apart from her or my babies." At that point, his diabetes had gotten so bad that it kept him from working even the most menial of jobs, and he lost all interest in caring for himself.

As he told his story, I could see his torture and agony. As he spoke of his family, he turned the wedding ring he still faithfully wore on his finger.

As he spoke of his family, he turned the wedding ring he still faithfully wore on his finger.

"I wished I could have been more attentive to my wife and had spent more time with my children. That would give me some comfort."

This was the harsh condition he was in when he began attending "our old church," as he called it. His divorce and separation from his family made him feel worthless.

The teaching at the church, however, comforted his broken

heart. Don had never heard the prophecies of Christ so well presented. He looked forward to every service, but never was able to develop close ties with anyone.

Don with his daughter, Patricia Toney Delong, during his last Christmas.

"People looked at me and wouldn't come any closer," he said. "They saw my outward appearance and maybe never considered that I was someone's child, husband, and father—just like anyone else. I doubt they knew that I once was able to work and contribute."

During one church service, Don couldn't stay in his seat any longer and went up to the altar. The pastor stepped from behind the pulpit and leaned toward him as the invitation hymn played. Don told him that he wanted the fullness of Christ in his life. He wanted the abundant life again.

The pastor told him to confess his depravity and his filthiness. "Tell the Lord," he said, "how mean you are."

Don wanted to say, "Why don't you tell Him how mean you are?" but he didn't. Instead, he turned and walked away.

There might have been a time when Don could have ignored these cruel words, but in his broken state, the words crushed his spirit. He no longer felt worthy to receive anything good from the Lord.

Don never went up front to the altar again. The words of his pastor took root in his heart, and their dark message seized his imagination. From then on he sat in the back of the church and left quickly at the end of every service. Whenever he thought of the Lord, he saw Him as a God of judgment whom he had to appease with good works.

Eventually Don withdrew further from the church and began searching the Scriptures to discover the true person of Christ.

"After I lost everything," Don said, sobbing, "I ran to Jesus and made Him my companion."

Don and I had gone to the same church during different periods and under the leadership of different pastors, but apparently he had experienced the same spirit of condemnation that I did. Different people were serving in and guiding the church, but the atmosphere never changed, at least not for me. I'd left when I was a resilient fifteen-year-old who wanted to pursue sports. Don had been a frail, broken man fleeing the pastor's portrayal of a harsh, hateful God. I was able to move on unscarred, but not Don. Don's experience reminded me of the trials set against Job.

"Do you see, son?" Don asked, struggling to contain his crying. "I believed another man's lie about the Lord. It's just like little crippled Mephibosheth believing the lie about King David. He was afraid of him until he understood that King David had a covenant with his father. Once he saw the truth, he ate at David's table as one of the king's sons."

"I know that my pastor and all the people loved each other back then," I said. "But I guess their love for the institution and doctrine sometimes took precedence over their love for each other."

"Yes, son."

"But the leaders and members of the church seemed to have such an incredible understanding of the scriptures."

"Many read the Living Word and understand all the prophecies," Don said, "but if they don't see Jesus and His love for His Bride, they're not reading it right."

It finally struck me why no one remembered much about Don. People never took the time to know him. His appearance seemed too much of an offense for them to become involved with him. If people could not see the value in Don, then they could not see Don. I understand how his appearance could make others uncomfortable, but how could they not be drawn to him immediately upon speaking with him? I thank the Lord that his appearance was never an issue with me. If I had allowed it to be an obstacle, my marriage would have disintegrated. And I'm convinced my whole life would have been ruptured from that loss. The Lord had sent me an unusual anointed provision in the person of Don.

If I had allowed Don's appearance to be an obstacle, my marriage would have disintegrated.

My schedule at the store was from 9 a.m. to 7 p.m. six days a week, so I rarely was able to get away. I usually arrived at 8 a.m. to spend some solitary time in prayer. Then I'd call Don just before I opened the store.

My cousin Randy was a tremendous help. Many times after working his city refuse route, he'd come into the store to help me. I never had to direct him on what to do; he'd go straight to stocking items, cutting meat, sweeping the floors, and delivering groceries. He was one of the hardest workers I've even seen, yet he refused to take a penny for all of his time.

His work ethic was exceeded only by his uncanny ability to make quick friends. If a customer came into the store and said, "It's sure hot outside," he'd say, "Well, it's cool in here. Why don't you let me buy you a pop?" On cold days he'd buy the customers coffee. Then they'd stand in front of my counter talking for as long as the customer chose to hang around.

Children couldn't get past Randy before he'd confront them with, "I bet you like cherry-flavored suckers" and a quick toss of a candy in their direction.

I was looking forward to the day when he came in while Don was there.

One evening just before closing, I received a delivery call from one of my regular customers, Velma, an elderly woman living in the nearby low-rent high-rise where Randy's mother, my aunt, also lived. After taking the order and hanging up the phone, I realized I had an appointment with my lawyer friend Mary, who was going to help me with some of the details surrounding the civil suit.

Randy wasn't available that night, and I was there alone with Don.

"I don't know how I'm going to handle this," I said to myself as I began pulling cans of vegetables off the shelf.

"What's the problem, son?" Don asked.

"I took an order from Velma before I realized I have an appointment directly after I close."

"I don't mind making the delivery for you."

"Are you going in that direction?" I asked.

"It's all right. I'd be glad to do it."

I stopped boxing the groceries. "Are you sure? She lives in the high-rise."

"Of course I'm sure. I'll help you box up everything."

I divided the groceries into three different boxes to keep the weight light for Don. When we carried everything outside, I realized I had never been close enough to look inside his car. There was no room to place the items. His backseat and floor were full of empty cans that he had picked out of dumpsters and along the street to earn money from the aluminum. Even with the windows open, the stench of all the liquids that had dripped over the worn upholstery and into the floors was overpowering. It was a sickening potpourri of beer, soda, and vegetable juice. When I saw the water jugs in the passenger seat, I remembered he didn't have running water. It was his habit to carry it all back to his shack for drinking and bathing. A lunch plate, still damp with ketchup, rested on the dash.

"Is your trunk empty?" I asked.

"No, son, it's quite full," he said. "Just put them on top of everything."

He set his box through the open window and I heard a number of cans spill onto the floor. I turned some of the cans on their sides before I stacked the other two boxes.

After Don got behind the wheel, he asked, "What about the money?"

"Just bring it in tomorrow," I said.

The next morning Don came in smiling. "Anytime you need help, just let me know. I made a good friend yesterday."

"And who would that be?" I asked.

"Velma," he said as he handed me a check from his delivery. "That lovely lady even gave me a tip."

He offered to give me the extra money, but I shook my head. "That's yours, Don."

"That Velma really is a sweet lady."

"Is she married?" I asked, knowing full well she wasn't.

"No, she's a widow."

"Uh-oh, Don," I said, teasing.

"No, no, not like that, son." When Don laughed, I could tell he enjoyed the ribbing.

We both got quiet and then laughed again.

"You know, son, I just loved her voice."

CHAPTER Five

Even though Leesa and I had promised each other that we would actively choose to let our ongoing struggle make us stronger, I still was overwhelmed with guilt over my sin. I never denied my responsibility for my actions; that was never the issue. My problem was fully believing that Christ had forgiven me for my wrongdoing. I'd feel His freedom for a few days, but then something like a notice for a delinquent bill or some mindless remark from a well-meaning friend would sink me. I reacted this way because the first thought that came to mind was, *If I hadn't mucked up everything, I'd be able to pay bills and not be placed in the position of hearing such comments.* Nothing seemed to help me escape my condemned state—not even Don's continual instruction to keep my eyes on what Jesus had already done for me on the cross.

As I sat alone in the store one afternoon, thumbing through my mail, I came across a note from the energy company threatening to cut off our electricity if we didn't pay immediately. The grocery store wasn't drawing in a lot of money, but the sales almost paid our bills. Then other money would come to us just in the nick of time from friends, family, and sometimes undisclosed givers. My head knew that all our needs were being met and that I would somehow be able to pay the electric bill, but the financial struggle was a constant reminder of my sin. I just couldn't stop kicking myself for making choices that had brought my family to this predicament.

Don's advice was correct about overcoming a series of bad decisions by making a series of right decisions. This made sense, but did not assuage my guilt.

I pushed the delinquent notice back into its envelope and let my mind drift back to the time my mother taught me how to confront bad decisions.

When my cousin Gene and I were ten years old, we came up with the foolish idea of stealing tomatoes from a neighbor's garden and throwing them at passing cars. Luckily our aim was off just enough so that we only hit one automobile. The woman slammed on the brakes, and we ran between the houses to escape down the alley. When we busted through my back door, Mom knew by our guilty expressions that we were up to no good.

"What have you been doing?" she demanded.

"Nothing." I stood still, fully believing she had some extraordinary powers that equipped her to read my mind. Gene must have believed the same, because he rushed home as quickly as possible.

"Let's go, Kevin," Mom said, nodding her head toward the front door.

I was dumbfounded and walked in front of her to the front porch. Somehow she had signaled my father, who was sitting in the living room reading the paper, and he joined us.

"Now, Kevin," she said, pointing to one of the chairs, "we're just going to sit here and wait for a while."

"Wait for what?" I asked, struggling to look innocent.

"Sit," she said.

I sat down with my parents and waited quietly for only a few minutes. When a police car began slowly circling the block, I broke down and confessed my crime. I never did figure out how she knew the authorities were coming, but this experience kept me on my toes for the remainder of my youth.

My parents explained to me the inappropriateness of my act and the trouble I had caused the lady driver. When I told them I was sorry, they forgave me, as did the lady, to whom I also gave an apology.

I never was confronted by the police, much to my delight. However, to right my wrong, I carried a bucket and a jug of laundry soap to that woman's house and washed her car. She was sweet, explaining that she understood how young boys can sometimes make silly decisions. "You need to learn from this," she said, handing me a glass of lemonade as proof of her forgiveness.

Despite the confirmation that everyone had forgiven me, I still felt condemned. I was facing the consequences of my act by washing the car, but with every swipe of my sponge, I was still the criminal.

It struck me as I sat at the counter in my store that I was in the same state as that silly ten-year-old who was already forgiven but who just would not accept it.

Whenever I managed the store or spent time with my family, I desperately tried not to be swallowed up in guilt because it completely shut me down. During this period I heard much about God's love and regard for me at an evening Bible school that I attended with Randy, but I still felt unworthy to fully embrace it. I kept reading scriptures about the Lord's forgiveness and the completeness of His death, burial, and resurrection, but I still fought my internal battle.

Leesa had a different struggle, for which I was absolutely no help. She constantly suffered with what other people thought of me and of her. I sometimes became impatient and wanted to tell her to toughen up, but I thank God that I never was that direct. I couldn't be, because I was the one who had caused all these problems for her. She was the innocent victim caught in the crossfire of my sin. I tried to explain logically the

Leesa had a different struggle, for which I was absolutely no help.

consequences of her worry, even though I felt I had no right to advise her. As it had been since the beginning, my impatience with her was rooted in my own guilt.

The tension between us peaked the day she came home from the post office in tears. When she mentioned running into an old friend of mine who had abandoned us after the newspaper exposure of the civil suit against me, I knew the chance meeting could not have been good.

"He just had to go on and on about the success of his new business," she said.

"People like sharing good news," I said, hoping to persuade her that his crass boasting was not intentional. But I knew better, because I knew the character of the man.

"Oh, no," Leesa said. "He knows about our struggle and enjoyed flaunting it in my face."

"Lee, you can't keep worrying about what other people think and say."

She continued, as if she hadn't heard me: "After picking up one of his large checks, he read the amount out loud and smiled."

"People are fickle. You'd better start accepting that this can happen again and again."

"It's really something when close friends of many years not only abandon you when you fall, but also enjoy your defeat."

"We're not defeated, Lee," I said.

"Well, today it feels like we are."

"I know, and you might feel that way tomorrow," I said. "If you keep worrying about other people, you're going to stay upset." I tried not to show my impatience with her, but the tone of my voice gave it away.

Leesa didn't answer. She sat down in a chair and looked across the room past me. She has never been one to argue or even raise her voice. And she was never one to feel sorry for herself and pout. But she was fragile during this time and had a broken spirit.

The next day I was still thinking about Leesa's upset over the post office situation. Usually I would be reading the Scriptures or listening to a sermon on the TV as I waited for customers, but this particular day I was just feeling beat over Leesa's ongoing struggle. Even though I had created everything that contributed to her problem, I just couldn't stifle my anger toward her. I wanted to show her that she was wasting precious time on people who didn't care. I was already past this kind of fear, so I thought it was time for her to be finished with it also.

What triggered my thoughts in this direction was receiving yet another delinquent bill notice. If I hadn't been so down, I could have almost laughed at the amount the company was demanding before they discontinued our service. Compared to the cost of a criminal lawyer, which I'd be paying if I was indicted on criminal charges, my bill with the late fee was truly insignificant. However, at that moment I didn't have the money to pay it.

It was one of those days when I felt like disappearing. I didn't want to talk about Leesa's worries or my ongoing cycle of guilt with anyone, even Don. However, I knew that Don would be arriving soon since he was now delivering groceries for me most every day.

When he came in that afternoon, I was reminded that I never could hide my feelings from my old friend.

He gave me his tithe to take to church, as was his habit ever since he became my regular employee. Then, looking intently into my face, he asked, "What's wrong, son?"

I explained to him about Leesa's confrontation at the post office and my impatience with her.

"I'm sorry to hear this," he said. "Leesa is carrying too large of a burden. Anytime we try to prove ourselves to others, we make others our potter, and we become the clay in their hands."

"Anytime we try to prove ourselves to others, we make others our potter, and we become the clay in their hands."

"I never thought of applying that particular passage in that way."

"Think about it, son. When people worry about the thoughts of others, they're revering man and not the Lord. This is why Leesa suffers with fear."

Don closed his eyes and prayed, "Help Leesa and Kevin to trust in You and not fear man, which ensnares them." Then, opening his eyes, he said, "Son, your relationship with Leesa parallels your relationship with Christ. Jesus provides us with true security. As this becomes more real to us, we in turn honor Him."

"I understand," I said, but in truth, I couldn't see the connection he was making.

"Women need security; men desire to be honored," he continued. "A man must first provide security for his wife and children before he can be honored."

"How can I provide any security, when I can hardly pay the bills? And I definitely won't be able to support her if I end up going to prison."

"You provide security by loving her when she's afraid," he said. "You can't expect her to process everything at the same time as you."

"I do love her," I said.

"Then listen to her and quit trying to change her," he said. "Do you know what happens once we understand God's perfect love for us?"

"What?"

"We are no longer afraid. We rush to Him and honor Him. If you love Leesa more selflessly, it will cast out all her fears," he said. "This is how you give her security."

"I guess without using the words, I was still communicating to Leesa to toughen up and change," I said.

"People don't make bad decisions when they're calmly trying to work out their problems. They make them when they're upset and operating in the flesh," Don said. "You see, son, you're responding out of anger or pain or fear."

He took my hand and pressed it to his chest and cried. His prayer was almost unintelligible through his sobs. "Draw Kevin's eyes to you, dearest Lord, draw his and Leesa's eyes to You."

I wouldn't fully comprehend the power of what Don prayed until much later, but until then, I traveled by the light I had at the time. Thereafter, I started listening to Leesa more and stopped playing the role of a corrective teacher.

I waited a few days before I told Leesa about my conversation with Don. She said she had already noticed the change in me; however, her plague of worry didn't suddenly disappear. Instead, her moments of fear rose and receded like waves on a beach, and finally over time, began to return less and less.

Over the next few weeks, I began receiving phone calls at the store for Don. Sometimes it was a man, sometimes a woman, but the callers never gave their names. "Is Don there?" the person would ask. When I said that he hadn't arrived yet, he or she would thank me and hang up.

One morning a man calling for Don took the time to add, "That Don is really something else."

"In what way?" I asked.

"I mean, he knows the Bible better than anybody."

"Yes," I said. "He's taught me quite a bit."

"That's because he knows the Bible," the man said. "We can hardly wait for our next study meeting."

"Don's leading a Bible study group?"

"Yes," the man said. "Tuesday and Thursday evenings at our high-rise."

I was so struck by this that I just held the phone without saying anything.

"When Don comes in, can you tell him that Jack called?" the man asked. "My doctor's appointment has changed to next week."

"Sure," I said.

As the man kept talking, I realized that Don was not only conducting Bible study groups in the high-rise; he was also picking up prescriptions for the elderly tenants and driving them to their doctor's appointments. After I hung up the phone, I couldn't help wondering how Don squeezed his friends into his packed car.

Don's Bible.

Later in the afternoon, I received a call from Velma. I grabbed a pen and pad to take her order but realized she was actually calling to speak with Don. I wasn't too surprised to learn that she was also attending his Bible study group.

"He's very knowledgeable," she said. "He has helped me learn so much."

When Don finally arrived, I saw he was carrying a worn red Bible, the spine held together with two overlapping strips of duct tape.

"Hello, Don." I held out my hand and asked, "Can I see your Bible?"

"Sure, son."

When I took it in my hands, I was thrilled. Here was the Bible in which he had spent hours searching for the true Christ. By its worn and ragged appearance, one wouldn't know of the hidden beauty and treasures within its pages. The cover was scarred and cracked with brittle, jagged edges. Originally a solid red, it had faded into a spotty rust color. Some sort of label on the upper half had been removed, tearing away pieces of its thin skin.

I opened the Bible and saw Don's messy scrawl of notes all over the wrinkled pages. It looked as though he had marked verses with whatever writing utensil was at hand: a pencil, a pen, a felt-tip marker. He had also highlighted long passages in yellow. It was the evidence of a man poring over every word and phrase, searching the heart of his Father.

I handed the Bible back to Don and said, "I guess I should start scheduling the deliveries around your Bible study meetings and your taxi service."

He looked at me in surprise and then said, "Yes, son, I've made some very dear friends at the high-rise."

"Well, you got two messages today," I said. "Jack's doctor's appointment has changed to next week."

"Okay. What's the other message?"

"It was more of a compliment than a message," I said. "In fact, a compliment came from two of them. Jack said you know the Bible better than anybody, and Velma said you have helped her learn so much."

> **"When you know God loves you and that He's been good to you like He's been to me, you just can't help but to give it away."**

Don smiled. "Well, when you know God loves you and that He's been good to you like He's been to me, you just can't help but to give it away."

It wasn't long before I learned that his elderly friends were no longer using the county senior citizen van service. Don had become their sole means of travel.

THE FIRST SEVERAL MONTHS after meeting Don, I didn't know why he took so long to enter my store. One afternoon after he drove up on his usual section of the sidewalk, I waited until I heard his door slam, and then went outside. I found him sitting on the front of his hood, staring at the hill that stood high above a cluster of homes across the road. It was the middle of October, and the fall colors had peaked to brilliant hues of red and yellow.

"Hello, Don," I said.

He remained seated as he bent his head toward me. "Hello, son."

"What are you doing?"

"Just taking time to enjoy the day," he said. He turned back toward the hill. "The Lord's handiwork is better than any painting we can produce."

"That's right, Don." I looked inside his car and saw that he had moved all the water jugs on top of his cans in the backseat, apparently making room for the new friends he now chauffeured.

Then I caught sight of another Bible resting on his dash. It was black but just as worn as his red one. The spine was repaired in the same way, with two messy strips of overlapping duct tape. A split ran from the bottom of the front cover halfway up the middle. I reached through the window, picked it up, and opened it. I saw that it too was marked up with notes and highlights, just like the red one. I wondered if he'd notated passages with the same comments.

"You ever take time, son, just to enjoy the masterpieces the Lord creates in the sky?" he asked.

I walked around the car and sat beside him. We must have sat together for ten minutes, not saying anything, just looking at the trees with their varying colors and the soft white clouds slowly drifting above them. I've often thought about that brief moment with my friend and have always been thankful I took the time to join him.

For months, Randy had wanted to meet Don. He had seen him often but only at a distance from the city garbage truck. Since he loved reading the Scriptures, he desperately wanted to meet this spiritual teacher of mine. Because of Randy's sense of humor, I sometimes couldn't resist telling him as he came into the store, "You just missed him. Try again tomorrow."

Finally, one day when Randy arrived, Don was sitting in his place in front of the ice cream freezer. When Randy saw him, he paused in the doorway and grinned.

"Here's my good friend Don I've been telling you about," I said. When Don stood up, I told him Randy was my cousin.

"Yes, I remember seeing you," Don said to Randy. "You're the city worker, aren't you?"

"That's right," Randy said. "I'm trying to keep this town from stinking."

When they both laughed, I knew a friendship had begun. I wasn't certain whether Don, caught off guard by Randy's sudden entrance and my quick introduction, just didn't have time to stress over meeting someone new, as he had done in the past. However, after the introduction, I saw that their connection was more than just the result of Randy's gift for quickly drawing a person into a place of comfort and familiarity. It was also Don's warm heart and appreciation of people that bonded the two. I sat back and let them talk without interrupting. To the customers who came into the store, they must have sounded like lifelong friends.

Ever since I had begun managing my store, Randy was a regular helper, but he wasn't the only one. His daughter Tiffany would sometimes operate the cash register so I could leave to pick up supplies or simply take a few minutes to drive around the block for a break. These brief moments away from work made a big difference for me.

My greatest helper, of course, was Leesa, who was there with me as much as possible. Her schedule was difficult, since she was both working and taking care of our daughters, but she came every Saturday and many evenings during the week to clean. She always brought Lindsey and Lauren. She encouraged our girls, calling them her best little workers, when in truth it was an added chore just keeping them focused and entertained. Nevertheless, I was always surprised how much Leesa was able to accomplish. I was happy to have all three of them near me.

One Saturday they worked into the afternoon, just long enough for me to hear the rumbling of Don's red Buick pulling up beside the store.

I called out to Leesa, who was nearby dusting shelves: "Guess who's here?"

"What is it?" Leesa asked, walking up to my counter. Lauren came just behind her, guiding her little sister by the hand.

"Guess who's just arrived?"

"Who . . . ?" Before I could answer, Leesa suddenly said, "Don!"

When Don came through the door, he stopped at the sight of Leesa and the girls.

"Don," I said, "this is Leesa and our babies, Lauren and Lindsey."

Don took the longest time looking into each of their faces. "It's a real pleasure to finally meet Kevin's sweet family," he said.

"Well, we've heard a lot from Kevin about you, Don," Leesa said. "And we couldn't be happier meeting you."

I could clearly see that Don was stressed—the way he was every time he met someone other than a child, an elderly person, or someone living on the street. I was sure Leesa saw it too, but it didn't inhibit her from expressing her usual warmth and graciousness. She appreciated Don not only because of all that I had said about him, but also because of the kind of person she is. His unattractive appearance was never a matter of concern for her. No one could talk with Leesa for long before sensing her sincerity and her heartfelt acceptance of them.

Within minutes, Don seemed as relaxed around Leesa as he was around me.

Don leaned down to Lauren and Lindsey and asked them, "Do you know what I can see?"

"What?" Lauren asked.

"I can see you both have been blessed with your mother's eyes."

"You can?" Lauren looked at Lindsey for proof.

Don laughed and said, "Yes, and I can see your father in you too."

"Do you know what I can see?" Don asked. "I can see you both have been blessed with your mother's eyes."

Leesa stayed the rest of the afternoon, taking time to talk with Don. Just as it had been with Randy, it seemed as if they had been friends for ages. In a way, they already knew each other through me. The girls responded to him as all children did. They were captivated by his stories and his tender way of teasing. And since his chair was in front of the ice cream freezer, he couldn't resist lighting up their afternoon with treats.

Don never discussed the Bible with Leesa. He mostly talked about the blessings of family and "little ones." The peculiar part was hearing him talk about his own children. This was the first time I noticed that whenever he told stories about his daughters and sons, he mostly referred to them as if they were still very young. A passerby listening in would have thought they weren't much older than my daughter Lauren.

I enjoyed the rest of the afternoon, hearing Don's conversations with my wife and children. Sometimes when I talked with Leesa and the girls, I caught Don intently studying us. Knowing how he still missed his wife and regretted not having spent enough time with his family, I wondered if he was thinking of them. Maybe it saddened him as he watched us. We were a reminder of what he had lost. What he held so dear was now many years behind him.

CHAPTER

Six

One morning I heard the rumble of Don's car and looked out to see him park in his usual place on the sidewalk. After hearing him slam his door, I waited, knowing he would take a while before coming inside the store. When he finally appeared in the front, I didn't recognize him. He was clean-shaven and wearing a new outfit.

He pushed the door back twice as he made his usual slow entrance. With the bell still ringing above him, he stood flushed and embarrassed, like a little boy in his first set of Sunday clothes.

I didn't dare add to his anguish by making any comments. His hair was clean, cropped above his ears, and slicked back with pomade. He had even trimmed his gray-and-white beard. If it weren't for his old thick-framed glasses, children coming into the store for candy might have mistaken him for Santa Claus. He wore a bright-red flannel shirt and a pair of blue dress pants. His dilapidated brown shoes with their broken laces had been replaced with freshly polished black oxfords.

Before Don even reached his seat in front of the ice cream freezer, I could smell his cologne.

"Good morning, Don."

"Good morning, son."

"What's the weather doing out there?"

"Not too chilly for a November day."

We spent the next thirty minutes chitchatting about weather, customers, store items, talking about everything except his sudden change in appearance. It was the first time I felt uneasy around Don. It was like sending a self-conscious boy out on his first date, when one wrong word, even a well-meaning compliment, could send him running. I was sure that this metamorphosis was motivated by his attraction to Velma.

Apparently Don's feelings toward Velma were shared. I had noticed that Velma now called only when she knew Don would be there.

Velma was a wonderful lady who always stayed upbeat and carried an unusual soft place in her heart for people. Her kindness toward Don not only made him comfortable but fostered a friendship that gave him something to look forward to. He knew he would be delivering groceries to her at least twice a week and that there would be times he could answer her calls about incoming items.

Eventually Don began taking longer and longer with his deliveries. It got to the point where I started becoming concerned. I didn't mind him taking his time, but I was worried about his health and him possibly having a wreck in his old Buick.

"Where have you been, Don?" I asked one time when he should have been back an hour earlier.

"Oh, I was just completing the delivery," he said.

"I don't care how long it takes, Don," I said. "I just want to make sure you didn't have any trouble on the road."

"No, son," he said. "No trouble on the road."

"Okay," I said, not pushing it any further.

Another day when he hadn't returned after three hours, I finally called Velma.

"Velma, by any chance is Don there?"

"Yes, honey. He's here having coffee."

When Don got on the phone, he sounded like a kid who had just been caught in the wrong place by his parents. He kept going on and on about grocery items Velma needed and how she was still working up her list.

"It's okay, Don. I just wanted to make sure there wasn't any trouble. You've been gone for three hours."

"No, son," he said. "There's no trouble."

A few days following this phone call, Don came up with a plan that he thought would successfully conceal how much time he was spending with Velma.

Minutes before each departure, he began telling me, "I'm going to be late, son; I have to run some errands on the way back." Sometimes he had to visit a sick friend or pick up prescriptions for someone or make a run to the post office. With this cushion of extra time, I would never know just how long he was visiting Velma. And, of course, why would I ever call Velma again when he was most likely somewhere else? Don continued this approach for some time, so he had to come up with numerous places to go before returning to the store.

Don came up with a plan that he thought would successfully conceal how much time he was spending with Velma.

Although I always treaded lightly when joking with Don, Randy was quite the opposite. He was careful never to offend him, but he was much freer teasing Don, me, or anybody walking into my store. Sometimes his prodding could be jarring, but it was always taken in good fun.

So as Randy and Don became better friends, more opportunities for my cousin's teasing arose. This never seemed to put a strain on their friendship. In fact, they enjoyed each other's company so much that many times they chose to deliver groceries together when Randy's schedule with the city permitted. The deliveries to Velma, of course, were never shared.

Whenever the two did deliver together, Randy always drove.

He just couldn't stomach riding in Don's car because of the mess and the smell.

Don knew the reason Randy would never ride with him, but it never stopped him from asking, "Randy, how about letting me drive this time?"

"No, Don," Randy would say, "I don't believe there's enough room to fit me in there."

After a few times, I noticed Don smiling at Randy's answer. That's when I realized it was Don's way of poking fun at Randy.

Late one afternoon Velma called in an order before Don had arrived, so Randy and I boxed up the groceries and set them on the counter.

Don finally came in, pushing the door back twice with two harsh rings of the bell.

"I'm sorry—I didn't mean to startle everyone," Don said. "It's just me." He looked even more spruced up than usual. He had pressed his new flannel shirt, and his slacks held a nice crease down each leg.

His customary noisy entrance drew more attention to his appearance. Randy, leaning against the ice cream freezer and sipping his coffee, just couldn't resist the opportunity. "Well, look at Don," he said, "looking all dapper."

"Now, now, Randy," Don said.

When Randy saw Don looking at the box of groceries sitting on the counter, he said, "Sorry, but you're too late; Kevin already set me up to deliver to Velma."

Don glanced at me and then back at Randy. He tried to answer, but stumbled over his words.

"I'm just kidding, Don. Don't get all flustered." Randy laughed so hard he had to hold his coffee at arm's length not to spill it on his shirt.

I couldn't help laughing too, after seeing Don's expression.

"You already got that territory marked," Randy added.

This statement from anyone else would have completely embarrassed Don. Instead, Don laughed out loud. "Oh, Randy!"

During these brief moments with Randy and Don, it was easy for me to forget myself and not obsess over what was yet to come my way with the lawsuit and possible imprisonment. But I didn't realize until years later just how much these times meant to me. I suppose the customers who were privy to this lighthearted bantering might have considered it simply cute and insignificant, but I knew better. I was watching Don, broken and guarded for so many years, now slowly disassembling his walls of self-preservation brick by brick. One afternoon, when both Randy and Don were at the store, I witnessed another layer of Don's defenses falling away.

The three of us were discussing a verse from the scriptures, which seemed to be the ultimate direction for most of our conversations. Randy, leaning against the ice cream freezer with his cup of coffee, and I, sitting behind the counter, were asking Don a number of questions. We were so lost in our discussion that customers entering the store felt more like interruptions.

Seeing a young man approaching the front door, Randy joked, "There goes our conversation; I bet you this guy will want some meat cut."

"Then I'll have to take time to ring it up," I said.

"And then what if he wants Don to deliver it?" Randy asked.

Don laughed with us. Just as the young customer came into the store, Don looked out the window and his face froze. Outside, Benedict—in his sunglasses, jacket, and frown—was marching quickly toward us.

Don stood up to make his usual getaway, but Randy pressed his hand on his shoulder. "Hold on there now. It's about time you quit your jackrabbit escape from Benedict. He's not a bad fellow."

Don slowly eased back down into his chair.

Instead of moving back to the counter to cut Benedict's order of bologna, I stayed to see what Randy was up to.

Before Benedict made his usual turn toward the Robitussin, Randy stopped him at the entrance. "Every week you come in here buying cough syrup," he said. "Who's it for?"

"My wife," Benedict said. He cocked his head at Randy as if he was trying to figure out why he was asking.

"Is the bologna for her too?" Randy asked with a smile.

"No," Benedict answered, still frowning. "The bologna is for me."

"You never share, huh?"

"I don't touch her cough syrup," Benedict said, "and she doesn't touch my bologna."

To my surprise, Don got caught up in this good-humored teasing and said, "Some people think bologna is good, unless you're full of it."

Benedict turned and stared at Don for a long time. "On second thought," he said, "maybe the bologna *is* for her."

Don and Benedict laughed so hard that both Randy and I couldn't stop laughing with them. It was the beginning of another friendship for Don. He never again fled when Benedict showed up at the store. Instead, the two men always took time to chat and laugh together. Benedict never changed his sunglasses or his jacket, but his scowl disappeared into a smile whenever he talked with Don.

"On second thought," Benedict said, "maybe the bologna *is* for my wife."

Not just Benedict but a number of my other customers were drawn into our conversations. They might have initially been in a hurry to pick up some items, but Randy would break their pace with his grin and his usual offer of a coffee or Coke. And, of course, he always bought the children candy. After my cousin's generous gift, the customers would stand in the front of the store talking with us, sometimes for as long as an hour. Don was the one, however, who remained the champion with children, leaning down to talk with them face-to-face.

Sometimes during these busy moments, I would slip outside to fill the pop machine. Since Don's Buick was always parked on the sidewalk, I barely had enough space between his car and the outside wall to carry the cans of soda. I always took the opportunity to toss a deodorizer through the open windows of Don's car or to spray the insides with a heavy mist of air freshener.

When I'd finish and walk back into the store, Don would ask, "What are you doing out there, son?"

"Filling the pop machine."

"And what else?" Don would ask, trying to hide his smile, knowing full well I was trying to refresh his car.

Then Randy would incite everyone's laughter with a statement like, "I hope that deodorizer was big enough to do the job."

The greatest part of all this carefree joking was watching Don slowly open up to more and more strangers who walked into the store. He was becoming less self-conscious and no longer retreated down an aisle to avoid contact with those he found intimidating.

Over time, the increasing number of phone calls told me that Don's Bible study groups, as well as his free taxi service, were expanding. People would call to tell him the time of their next doctor's appointment or let him know that new guests would be coming to his meetings. My earlier joke about having to schedule the deliveries around his Bible classes and taxi service was becoming a reality.

WHAT INITIALLY STARTED as Don's friendly gesture to deliver groceries so I could keep my appointment with Mary, my lawyer friend, had developed into a steady position in which Don was really helping me. Most amazing was seeing how the Lord took that small decision and multiplied the results. There was no way I could have foreseen how this was going to lead Don into developing relationships with Velma and his friends at the high-rise apartments. I never would have dreamed that the Lord would use all this to bring Don to the place where he could be completely free to express who he really was.

One afternoon Don came in the store and asked me, "Do you have the order ready?"

"What order?"

Don hesitated, looking a little embarrassed, as if he had overstepped himself. "I just thought you might have an order already."

"No, there hasn't been any order. Why would you think that?"

The phone rang, and Don's face flushed a deep red. When I answered the call, it was Velma needing groceries. I wrote down the list of items, hung up the receiver, and handed Don the order.

"I guess you were right," I said, smiling. "Velma needs a few things."

Don looked away as he took the list. "I guess I'll get all this together for her."

He was much like a shy teenager trying to hide his blossoming relationship from me. Of everything he and I had ever discussed, this seemed to be his most sensitive area. I was also struck by the shift in Don's sense of responsibility concerning the store. In the beginning, he avoided any appearance of being an employee. He always refused to cut meat for the customers or even stand behind the counter. Whenever he answered the phone, he would lean across the counter to hold the receiver. I never asked him to explain this. For a while, I thought he feared that his disheveled looks would dishonor me and my business; but then he continued to keep his distance even after he had cleaned up his appearance. For Don to check with me about Velma's order showed, for the first time, that he was taking ownership of his position. I knew this was the beginning of a change that went beyond Velma, and over the next weeks I was going to watch it come into complete fruition. It was no longer simply me learning of the orders and sending him out for deliveries. He was now a permanent fixture in my business, privy to the needs of our customers, who were placing more and more orders directly with him.

After Don boxed up Velma's order, I said, "Don, I have an idea."

"What's that, son?"

"Since you talk a lot with Velma, why don't you just let Velma tell you her order?" I said. "Then just give me a heads-up, so we won't be caught off guard next time."

"That sounds like a good idea," he said.

I could tell he was happy with the change. This arrangement made way for what he was doing already and would dispel his concerns about beating me to the orders. At the same time, it gave him the freedom to serve his friends without having to go through me.

Don's plan of running "personal errands" when he delivered to Velma was beginning to wear thin. I could tell he struggled to come up with enough places to cover the long hours spent visiting his friend. The whole arrangement was amusingly absurd, but I went along with it. Then Don came up with an even better plan.

"Son, do you mind if I deliver after you close?" he asked. "I'll bring the customer's check in the next day."

"That's fine with me, Don." I knew very well that he was only talking about deliveries to Velma. This meant he could spend the whole evening with her, and I would never know. It was amazing how this brainstorm of his completely took away his embarrassment—all because it made his sweet relationship with Velma more private.

Don's relationship with Velma was more than simple friendship, but I knew he would never allow it to turn romantic. To the end of his days, he would always mourn the loss of his wife, never removing the wedding band from his finger.

Don's relationship with Velma was more than simple friendship, but I knew he would never allow it to turn romantic.

Since Don felt no more pressure to cover up his time spent with Velma, I was able to tease him more freely.

One evening at closing, as Don was gathering Velma's order, I said, "You're spending more time at Velma's apartment than at my store."

"Well, she's a good customer," he said.

"Maybe," I said with a quick wink, "I should start sending Randy down there to deliver?"

"Oh, I wouldn't do that," Don said, blushing. "No, I wouldn't do that at all."

CHAPTER

Seven

I KNEW THE LORD had sent Don into my life with a definite purpose. In fact, I sensed that the Lord had drawn us together to transform both of our lives. Leesa felt the same way, but one evening she became more expressive about my friendship with Don.

"Think about the Lord's divine intervention in all of this," Leesa said. "Don came into your life just three weeks before the civil lawsuit."

"I agree, Lee. I could never have planned something like this."

"Think of this too," Leesa said. "Both of you understand how people can twist the truth in Scripture, causing oppression and pain. You both know this because you come not only from similar church backgrounds but from the very same church."

"It really is amazing," I said.

"I thought of something else," Leesa said. "You would never have allowed yourself to open up to Don and see his worth if the Lord hadn't prepared you years ago."

"What do you mean?"

"From all the stories you've told me, most people just dismiss Don, never giving him a chance to share his life with them."

"That's right," I said. "Before he cleaned himself up, he was invisible to most people. They saw him as a street person, not a human being who could contribute something to their lives."

"My point is that your parents never consider outward appearances, and that made the way for you to accept Don," she said. She recalled the story about my father happily riding on the back of the city garbage truck after losing the bottling-plant manager's job. "Seeing this as a young boy showed you that outward appearances and the struggle to promote a particular image are empty. All of this had to prepare you for this day."

"I never thought of that," I said. I was bowled over by her words. It was proof again of God's wisdom and love in bringing everything together: my strengths, my weaknesses, the minute details of my personality and background. I couldn't help thinking how impossible it was for anyone to run from God. And considering the good He intends for us, who would want to?

In the months following my conversation with Don about Leesa's fears, I continued making every effort to simply love my wife through her struggles and not try to change her. In turn, as Leesa saw the Lord ministering to me through my friendship with Don, it was easier for her to focus more on God's guidance and less on what others were saying about our situation. However, she was always in public. In addition to her involvement with her school, she frequently took Lauren to various events. This exposure, coupled with her tender heart and unwillingness to cut off people, made her an open target for questions and careless remarks.

I made every effort to simply love my wife through her struggles and not try to change her.

It wasn't that Leesa was overly sensitive to every comment or inquiry about the lawsuit. Leesa, in fact, answered a number of questions from friends and acquaintances who sincerely wanted to know that she and her family were all right. However, there were certain people who seemed just plain curious and hungry for details. And a few of these inquiring folks couldn't help giving Leesa their perspective, which was almost always hurtful and misguided at best.

To successfully sidestep this kind of confrontation, Leesa began bringing Lauren to her ballet and her gymnastics classes only minutes before they began. If there was a picnic or park outing for the schoolchildren, she expertly positioned herself away from those who had grilled her in the past. If she had to sit with a group at a ball game, she made certain Lindsey was with her, which discouraged most people from pelting her with questions.

It would have been much easier if Leesa had simply pulled Lauren and Lindsey out of their activities, but Leesa and I both wanted to keep everything as normal as possible, especially for our daughters.

I saw the change in Leesa. She became less upset over the prospect of someone asking questions and more concerned about avoiding unproductive chatter.

Also, Leesa and I both felt that our discomfort with discussing my situation went beyond us. We were considering not only ourselves but also others. We didn't want to place anyone in the awkward position of not knowing what to say after they felt the obligation to broach the subject.

After a number of conversations with various people, Leesa and I discovered that most people don't know how to comfort others. Although sincere, many held perspectives that were limited by their experiences. Those who were focused on their own disappointments only expressed how negative life can be. And, of course, this counsel was never good for Leesa. Many people facing trials, even if self-made as in my case, are seeking the comforting presence of a sincere listener—not an advisor giving pat answers. Words alone cannot bring someone through a trial. People first need to hear the truth of God's love and forgiveness, and then they must process and embrace it.

But even though I knew God loved and forgave me, and even though I was learning so much from Don, I still could not accept the Lord's freedom from my guilt. Leesa and I had many conversations about who we were in Christ and how we needed to let Him use the catastrophe I had foisted upon us to transform our hearts, but none of this was sinking into *my* heart. The more I struggled, the more I recalled that day in the hamburger shop when Don told me that self-hate never grows into the abundant life.

This trap even inhibited me from sharing my testimony. It was easy to speak to my customers—they only knew me as the store owner who provided them with groceries. However, sharing with certain people who had known me before my fall was a whole different matter. I didn't feel inhibited by everyone—only those I thought had held high expectations of me. I was convinced they were disappointed in me because I had failed to uphold my prior reputation. After I was broken by my own doing and was now repentant, I was certain they watched me closely and expected me to be strong. I could never tip my hand, confessing to them that I still felt broken and like an utter mess.

I felt this way especially with two men whom I had met at church. I had known them for a while but after my wrongdoing saw them just long enough for brief conversations. However, what I did know of them was a little intimidating, considering my state of mind. They both led exemplary lives and were known for their faith even beyond the church. Whether in prayer meetings or at work, they never shifted from what they believed. They boldly practiced and shared their faith throughout the community. Anyone seeing how they carried themselves or watching their well-disciplined children would have to be impressed with both of them.

One Wednesday evening, Leesa couldn't attend church because of an event for Lauren, so I went by myself. After the prayer service, I ran into my two friends just as I was leaving the sanctuary.

"How is everything going, Kevin?" one of the men asked.

"Good," I said. The truth was, I felt much weighed down that evening.

"Well, it has to be hard for you at this time."

"It is," I said, "but things are going to get better."

"We're continually praying for you and your family," the second man said.

"I appreciate that," I said, but I really didn't like hearing it. I preferred talking about anything but my problems, especially with people who would never be able to relate. Talking in detail with Don, of course, was quite different; he knew what it was like to be broken. I wanted people at church to know my situation, but then I preferred not to have it brought up. Sometimes, when talking about other topics, I was able to forget my present trouble, even if for only a few minutes.

I struggled to hold up my image as a repentant Christian who was now strong and moving in the right direction.

But when someone said they were praying for me, I'd suddenly be reminded that I had strayed way off track. These comments forced me to think about my ongoing problems time and time again. On top of this, I struggled to hold up my image as a repentant Christian who was now strong and moving in the right direction. Giving quick replies that everything was going to get better was my attempt to prove it.

One of the men surprised me by saying, "I can certainly relate to what you're going through."

"You can?"

"I sure can," he said. "Sometimes it can be an uphill battle to forget past sins so you can face each day new." He went on to explain that he had lost everything because of his alcohol abuse. "I was newly married to a good woman and had my first real job, with a solid future."

"I had no idea," I said.

"Everybody looks their best in church," he joked. "I didn't plan to fall like I did. My addiction had escalated to where I started drinking on the job. I just couldn't stop, despite the fact that I lost my position and my marriage."

I was really taken by surprise by his story, and how open he was about it.

"After my conversion," he continued, "it took me a while to bury the old me."

"You mean your struggle with alcohol?"

"No," he said. "I had to free myself from thinking about the harm I had caused and move on like a new person in Christ."

"That's where I am now," I said. "I want to move on and face the consequences as a new man."

"You can," the other man said. "I didn't have a drinking problem, but my wrong attitude and anger destroyed my marriage. Before I finally accepted Christ's answer, I blamed everybody and everything for my troubles. The plain truth was that I destroyed everything good in my life piece by piece."

"How did the Lord change it for you?"

"The first thing He showed me was that I had become a new creature in Him. If you don't get this, you'll never restore and build back your life."

"You can be a new person in Christ and yet keep thinking like the old person who is already dead and gone," the first man said.

I knew what they had shared was true for me, but the significance of their words didn't really dawn on me until I was driving home. I had heard this many times from Don, but now I finally understood. The clarity came to me not so much because of how they conveyed their message but because of their willingness to share their past mistakes. I was struck by the revelation that everyone has his own story. Each man could have kept his past secret and I never would have guessed, but they weren't concerned about promoting a particular image. I was now convinced that they had seen right through my façade all along. Rather than guard their own reputations, they wanted to minister to another hurting Christian. Ultimately I learned that there is power and life in transparency, as long as it is bathed in wisdom.

These two men were able to abandon self-promotion, because

they knew that trying to live up to the expectations of others is hogwash. I had been trying to exhibit strength to these two men because I thought they viewed me that way. Now I realized they'd never had those expectations in the first place.

They were free from their guilt because they knew that Christ had renewed their lives. The reason my two friends were able to separate past from present was that they chose to talk openly about their pasts, never trying to lift up a false image of themselves. When I thought about our conversation, it dawned on me that each of them talked about his past as if he were discussing an acquaintance whose funeral he had attended. I knew then that talking about the "dead man" with others could separate me from my past. This distinction between the new man in Christ and the old buried man helped me see how differently God viewed me. Hating my old self could never sustain me, much less my family.

By the time I pulled up in our driveway, I felt released from my guilt. I was overwhelmed with peace and emotional freedom. I decided to wait until Leesa and I were alone at bedtime to tell her about my experience.

At home that evening, I hadn't gotten very far when Leesa interrupted me, saying, "Kev, I could see a difference in you the minute you came through the door."

The next morning I called Don from the store and told him how I was finally freed from my burden of guilt.

"This is exactly what I've been trying to say to you," he said, "but you weren't in a position to hear it."

I thought I understood what he meant, but wouldn't fully comprehend the depth of this statement until years later. I eventually came to understand that not being "in a position to hear it" meant that my heart wasn't broken enough to embrace the truth. And because of this, I couldn't accept Don's message no matter how clearly he had communicated it.

Not being "in a position to hear it" meant that my heart wasn't broken enough to embrace the truth.

I was obviously hurting during this period, but my heart wasn't yet open to this revelation because I was still struggling to uphold my reputation and strength through my own efforts. And an unbroken heart cannot receive truth. That particular evening at the Wednesday service, my weary heart couldn't resist the transparency of two compassionate friends. After this confrontation, I was immediately released from my burden of guilt.

When people appear to have their whole lives together without any glitches, it can only be a façade. Once I understood this, I was free of the continual struggle to prove myself to everyone. I had been criticizing Leesa for worrying about what others think, yet I was doing the same thing. I was worried they would see the real me, broken and afraid.

Don was the best example of someone who embraced this teaching. He was noticeably broken and had no trouble expressing his vulnerability. And he could genuinely suffer for someone else because he knew suffering firsthand.

Now that I was finally experiencing freedom from my guilt, I realized just how heavy my burden had been. I suddenly felt exhilarated, knowing I could face anything as long as the Lord was with me. This didn't mean I ignored my wrongdoing or that I wanted to escape the consequences of my sin. Quite the opposite was true. I was now even more determined to face my problem and accept what followed.

The burden of my sin had been lifted that January night I repented, but I had continued to hate myself, and I picked that burden up again and again. My guilt not only affected my relationship with Leesa and our girls, but it also tainted every good memory. I was so steeped in guilt and self-derision, I couldn't even reflect on my relationship with Leesa without feeling great pain and anguish. I couldn't stop thinking about how my wife could have been much better off had she chosen someone else. I had wronged her and my family in a way I knew would forever leave scars.

Once I completely accepted the truth that I was forgiven, I found myself freer to love my wife and daughters. Finally understanding the fullness of what Christ had done changed everything for me. To my surprise, I was immersed in sweet memories of my life with Leesa. Instead of haunting me with feelings of guilt and regret, these reflections now ushered in an overwhelming love and adoration for her.

Once I completely accepted the truth that I was forgiven, I found myself freer to love my wife and daughters.

I couldn't stop thinking about the first time I met Leesa at the local football stadium during my first year in college. It was as if that crisp fall afternoon, active with people cheering and meandering up and down the stands, was just a week ago. I hadn't even wanted to go to this game, but my friend Buddy had talked me into it. Buddy didn't know Leesa, but he knew the girl with her that evening, so he struck up a conversation with them.

I was immediately taken with Leesa. She was the kind of person who exuded purity and honesty from the very first words she spoke. There was nothing pretentious about her or any superficial attempt to impress me or my friend. Her wide-open blue eyes and easy smile let me know she was someone I could trust. I don't know how we enjoyed any kind of conversation amid the crowds clapping and rooting for their respective teams, but we did. After spending much of the game talking with her, I secured a date with her for the next Saturday.

During the week, however, I got back together with my old girlfriend from high school. When I called Leesa and broke off our date, she was sweet and understanding. I thought that was it—that I probably would never see her again—but the Lord had something else in mind.

Two years later I was working full-time for a finance company in my hometown while still taking classes in college. As a service rep, I made phone calls and completed applications. During December, the company needed me to fill in for a week at the branch office forty miles away. After I'd been at this location for just a couple of days, a coworker named Faith wanted to match me up with her sister-in-law. I was a little hesitant but asked to see a picture of her. When she showed me a photo, I almost reeled back. It was Leesa. Even in my startled state, I couldn't help noticing again how beautiful she was.

"This girl won't go out with me," I said, handing the picture back.

After I'd explained why, Faith told me not to worry about it. "I think you two should go out together," she said. "Just let me talk with her."

Leesa agreed to go to a Christmas party with me. After that party, our relationship blossomed. We were married within the year.

As I thought about all of this, I relished the fact that God didn't let me miss out on having Leesa as my wife. He wasn't limited by my lack of consideration when I broke off a date at late notice for the sake of rekindling an immature high-school relationship. How could it have been coincidence for me to work at an office with Leesa's sister-in-law two years later? Except for the Lord's influence, why else would this woman—whom I didn't know—arrange a blind date between me and Leesa?

Now released from guilt, not only was I able to love Leesa more fully, but I was free to think about her in the way the Lord intended—without the chains of all my personal baggage.

CHAPTER
Eight

"PEOPLE LIVING ON THE STREET WON'T GOSSIP," Don said to me one morning in the store.

"Why is that?"

"They know how it hurts because they are constantly shunned by society," he said. "Gossip cuts very deep, and they don't want to pass on that kind of destruction."

Most everything Don told me was surprising and new.

"That's not to say they're completely disconnected from all

that's going on in the community," he said. "In fact, they usually know more than most people."

"How could they?"

"You mean because they're living outside of the mainstream?"

"Well, yes," I said.

"Don't forget how they live. They're always out and about talking to people. They don't just stay within their own group."

"I guess they are probably talking about my case with the bank."

"Some are talking about it, but they never learned it from me," Don said. "Realize, son, they may not have the money for a newspaper, but they're interested enough to read the headlines through a dispenser window or pick up an old paper left on a bench."

"So what are they saying about my case?"

"They're discussing the details they know and are awaiting the outcome."

I was really astonished. "Why would they even be interested?"

"They know you as the corner grocer. Those who have never been in your store still feel like they know you through those who are your occasional patrons."

"I hate to admit it, but I never considered any of this."

"They know the exact day when you first started managing the store," Don said. "I don't encourage discussion about your personal business, but I have heard talk among them. None of it is critical or even comes close to gossip, and it never will."

"That's quite a contrast to what most people do."

As we were talking, a cab pulled up in front of the store, and the driver came inside.

"Driving day shift?" Don asked him, abandoning his usual shyness with adult customers.

"That's right." The man smiled at both of us. "You can't beat the peaceful shift of driving during the daytime."

"Day shift means transporting mostly senior citizens," Don said.

The driver looked directly at Don. "Do you drive a cab?"

Don laughed. "Not now, but I did years ago. Nothing like the freedom of moving all over town."

"That's why I got into it," the driver said. "I'd just waste away at a desk job."

"Are you always driving daytime?"

"Sometimes I drive nights," he said. "And that gets pretty rowdy with all the drunks."

"I remember those times," Don said. "During the day your destinations are grocery stores and doctor's appointments. At night you're moving between bars and nightclubs."

"You sure got that right," the driver said.

"We would say day shift was easy but never as exciting."

The driver laughed. "Only a fellow cabdriver knows this."

After the driver bought a cold soda, Don walked him to the door and waved good-bye. He stood at the window watching until the cab was out of sight.

I couldn't help wondering how much Don lived inside his memories. Whenever he discussed his wife and children or crossed the path of someone like this cabdriver, he seemed highly drawn to his past. His response was more than simple reminiscence. It hurt me to think that Don was at the end of his life and that I was benefiting from what he'd learned through loss. At times I felt he was investing all he had in me so that my life could prosper in all the areas his life could not.

It hurt me to think that Don was at the end of his life and that I was benefiting from what he'd learned through loss.

A few days after the cabdriver stopped in and just before Easter, I saw firsthand that my concern for Don was misplaced.

That morning, Velma called the store and said, "I guess you've heard the news."

"What news?"

"Don is moving into our high-rise."

"When did this come about?" I was amazed to hear the news. I had known Don for a year and never really considered the possibility of him moving into the senior citizen housing.

"It's been in the works for a while," she said, "but he's moving in this week."

"I had no idea. Don never mentioned it."

"Well, I'm sure he will want to tell you." It was impossible for Velma to conceal the delight in her voice.

When Don arrived that afternoon, he had another surprise. When he opened his mouth to speak, his wide smile displayed a set of brand-new teeth.

"Hello, Don." I was so taken aback by this change that I found myself struggling not to stare at his mouth. I knew for his sake not to take any notice of it. He was as self-conscious as a young boy whenever he changed anything to better himself, whether it was a haircut or a new shirt. This was the first time I realized that Don wasn't embarrassed about me seeing his personal changes as much as he was by my knowing what was behind them. We had become kindred spirits and couldn't conceal much from each other. No doubt he felt I knew his personal improvements had everything to do with befriending Velma.

Don sat in his chair in front of the ice cream freezer. "It looks like it's going to be a beautiful Holy Week," he said. "Easter is coming quick." Apparently his teeth still felt intrusive, for he lightly touched his mouth after each sentence.

"Yes, the weather couldn't be better," I said. "Velma called earlier."

"She did? Does she have an order?" He felt around his mouth again.

"No. She said there's some exciting news you might want to tell me."

Don hesitated, and then as if suddenly remembering, said, "You must mean me moving into the high-rise."

"That's right."

"I was content where I was," he said, looking embarrassed. "But all my friends wanted me in there, so I just went along with it."

I learned that day just how much his friends, especially Velma, wanted him living in the high-rise. After Don left to make a few deliveries, I talked with a couple of people in his Bible study group about how everything had transpired.

The lengthy waiting list for the senior citizen housing didn't deter his friends. Spearheaded by Velma, they'd launched a campaign to persuade the local housing authority to allow Don to become a tenant. Through numerous phone calls and letters, they'd emphasized Don's selfless service of picking up their prescriptions and taking them to doctor's appointments. This months-long crusade finally convinced the right people, who let Don bypass the waiting list and qualify as a tenant. Since the housing was subsidized low-rent for senior citizens, I knew his meager Social Security check would be just enough for him to afford it.

After hearing all of this, I knew how foolish it was to think of Don's life as being over. He had suffered much loss in his past, but it was obvious he was indeed building a new life for himself.

Around this time, I was seeking someone with influence to help me, namely a defense lawyer. I hadn't been indicted on federal charges yet, but I knew my parents were right about the importance of handling my situation responsibly. There was no question that I was going to openly confess my crime and accept the penalty, but to face prosecution without proper counsel would be unwise. I didn't care much about the consequences for myself, but I was greatly concerned for my family. What happened to me obviously affected them.

Up to this point I had been helped by my attorney friend, Mary. She was taking care of everything for the civil lawsuit without charging me. She was such a lifesaver, but not being a criminal lawyer, she couldn't help me if I was indicted on criminal charges.

My first thought was to retain a high-profile attorney with a great success rate. I found him in Frankfort, Kentucky. He was widely known across the state for his legal savvy. I felt I was in good hands with this man, especially after I met him. I made it clear that I wanted to be honest about my crime and accept the consequences.

He acquiesced to this and added, "What you don't want is conviction on unfounded charges."

"Yes, that's right."

"Then if we're in agreement, I'll be glad to represent you," he said. "For me to start, I'll need a retainer of twenty thousand dollars."

"For me to start, I'll need a retainer of twenty thousand dollars."

I was so surprised by this amount I couldn't respond. I had expected to pay quite a bit for his services, but not this much. He could just as well have asked for a million dollars, because both amounts were impossible.

"Are we in agreement?" he asked.

"I don't have that much money." Knowing that I would eventually have to secure a lawyer, I was holding on to some savings. Also, family and friends had been contributing for this purpose. Karen, my sister, was even skipping lunch at work and sending us the money. Some support came anonymously through another party. Occasionally Leesa would receive an envelope marked "For Legal

Fund." The amounts we received were large and small, but even collectively, they couldn't match this lawyer's fee.

We sat quietly for a few minutes, and then the lawyer broke the silence: "I'll give you two weeks to come up with the fee."

I needed a good lawyer for the sake of Leesa and our girls. I wanted to face what was coming to me, but I had read about cases where poor representation resulted in outlandish sentences. If I was facing prison time, I wanted someone who could return me to my family as quickly as possible.

In my desperation, I said, "I'll try to come up with the money."

When my parents, sister, and friends heard of my need, they all gave more for the retainer, despite having given so much already. Leesa continued receiving anonymous gifts as well. By the end of the two weeks, I had a lot more than I'd started with, but still not nearly enough.

When I called the lawyer and told him my total amount, he said, "This is not going to work."

"Can I pay as we progress through the case?"

"I'm afraid not."

After I hung up, I just sank. I was convinced that this man was the best choice for me because of his reputation and influence. I didn't know what to expect next. But from our conversation, I did know that as good as he was, he was all about business, with no flexibility for personal needs.

I called Leesa and told her the outcome.

"What are we going to do now?" she asked. "What do you think the Lord has in mind for us?"

"Lee, I don't know. I was convinced he was the Lord's choice for me."

"Call Mary," Leesa said.

"She's not a criminal lawyer."

"I know, but maybe she can guide you to somebody else who's good but not so expensive," she said. "You need a lawyer."

When I called Mary, she said she'd try to find somebody for me. "Let me do some searching," she said, "and I'll call you right back."

Next I called my parents. They both encouraged me not to worry.

"If we can't afford this particular lawyer," Mom said, "the Lord will bring someone else."

When I called Don and explained everything to him, he listened quietly.

After I had finished, he prayed, "I thank you, God, for your unique guidance through this. Help us rest in You and walk out Your plan, which You set in place before the foundation of this earth." Then he said, "Son, it's clear that the Lord doesn't want you to have that man as your lawyer."

"It just seemed so right," I said. "Lack of money is what killed it."

"No, son. You can't afford him because he's not the one."

"He's not the one," he said. "There's someone else."

"I know he's not the one because I can't afford him."

"No, son. You can't afford him because he's not the one. The Lord opens doors and always provides the way to go through those doors. He will never guide you to a certain point with no provision. The amount of that fee is too much for you in every way. It is an incredible burden."

"I guess in the end the main thing is that I just have to move on."

"What's most important is for you to see the Lord through this," he said. "He's not the right attorney, son, because God's not going to put something on you that you can't reach."

It finally struck me what he was saying. I had been so frantically trying to retain the best counsel that I had placed all my confidence in this one man. Don's words shook all of that loose. He helped me see God's guiding hand in all that was happening.

I had been so frantically trying to retain the best counsel that I had placed all my confidence in this one man.

An hour later, Mary called back. "I contacted a friend who put me in touch with a good attorney in Prestonsburg," she said. "I don't know what he'll charge, but he will be considerably less expensive. His office assistant is waiting for your call."

The assistant was nice and set me up for an appointment the next day. Before I got off the phone, she put me on the line with the attorney. Mary had apparently given him an overview of my situation.

The man had a quiet and almost reserved temperament, which was calming for me. I took the opportunity to ask how much he charged as a retainer. When he told me, I almost dropped the receiver. The amount equaled what I already had, thanks to the help of my family, friends, and anonymous givers.

After our conversation, I called Mary and asked her if she'd told the lawyer how much I had raised for a retainer.

"How could I?" she asked. "I never knew what you had."

I then called Leesa and told her about the new attorney and all that Don had shared.

"Do you realize that all of this has been worked out within two hours since you first called me?" she said.

"This is really amazing."

"What can we do now, Kev, but marvel at what the Lord will do next?"

"What can we do now, Kev, but marvel at what the Lord will do next?"

The following day, I drove to Prestonsburg to meet with my new lawyer. He had a much smaller office than the previous man. After his friendly assistant greeted me, I sat in a chair and looked about the room, glancing at the pictures on the wall and the modest décor. I realized immediately how I had been persuaded by the more impressive surroundings of the prior lawyer, but now I could sense that this was where I was supposed to be.

My first meeting with my attorney was brief. Even though he already knew the general details of my case, he wanted to hear all the specifics from me.

"As you know," he told me, "you haven't been indicted on criminal charges."

"That's right," I said. "Right now I'm just facing the civil suit."

"At this point, just the investigation is going on," he said. "As of now, we're not sure how the civil suit will end up. And we don't know there will even be a criminal case."

"So where do we go from here?"

"We wait," he said. "If it moves into a criminal indictment, I'll do all I can for you."

As I sat there, I thought about Don's prayer acknowledging the Lord's plan, which He had long before set in place. It was a plan God had made—not two weeks before, when I had talked to the first lawyer, but long before I was born, before the foundation of this earth.

CHAPTER

Nine

After several weeks of hearing nothing from my lawyer, I complained to Leesa. I told her I wanted to know what was going on so I could prepare. The truth was I just wanted to move everything forward as fast as possible. I never was good at sitting back and doing nothing. My natural tendency has always been to jump in and fix everything. Waiting for months between each step in this legal process was agonizing. Don often referred to it as a cloud that was always hanging over me.

"The last time you talked with him, he told you no criminal charges had been filed," Leesa said.

"Yes, I know, but that was two months ago."

"Don't you think he would have called if something has happened?" Leesa asked.

"Probably, unless he's too busy with other clients," I said. "I'm going to call and get an update."

Leesa gave me one of her looks, which clearly said, *You'd best just let the lawyer alone.*

Leesa was right. When I called my lawyer, he confirmed that nothing as of yet had transpired. "If anything happens," he said, "I'll contact you immediately."

"I want to talk with the prosecutor," I said.

"Why would you want to do that?" I could hear from the tone of his voice that this was an unusual request from a client.

"If I could just talk to him, we would know his intentions. This would equip us to move this case more quickly to its ultimate end."

"Absolutely not," he said. "I can't let you talk with prosecution."

"You would only make things worse by contacting him."

"Then will you contact him just to assess his plans for my case?"

"No," he said. "Don't you understand that no criminal charges have been filed?"

"Yes, I understand," I said.

"You would only make things worse by contacting him."

"But if he is considering filing charges, why keep waiting to talk with him?"

"We don't know for sure that he's going to indict you; it may remain just a civil suit," he said. "And with all of this in mind, I don't want to keep bringing up your name to him."

"Okay," I said. I was still revved up and wanted to talk to the prosecutor, but I deferred to my lawyer's seasoned expertise, at least for the moment. He and I had a few more similar conversations over the next few weeks.

Two months later, in August 1998, while my friend Mike was visiting me at the store, my lawyer called.

"I wanted to let you know," he said, "that a grand jury indicted you yesterday."

I was stunned. Despite my earlier impatience and efforts to gain some kind of control over the process, I was shaken upon hearing this. I wasn't completely ignorant of the legal steps, for I had been reading as much as I could on my own. However, this was all new to me—I'd never been in this kind of trouble or been down this path before.

"What's next?" I asked.

"I haven't gotten any papers yet," he said. "When I do, I'll send them to you. After you receive everything, call me." He wanted to make certain I understood that the federal indictment was completely separate from the bank's civil suit.

"Okay. But what happens? I mean, what can I expect to face over the next few days?"

"The time frame is not going to be days but months," he said.

"It's not a quick process." Then he walked me through the lengthy legal procedures, including the arraignment and all the hearings.

I was truly wrestling within myself. I wanted to pay my debt for what I had done and start my punishment soon, and yet I didn't want to be separated from Leesa and the girls. And the more I saw how long the process took, the more I wondered if I could endure the wait. I knew I had no right to complain. Whatever the process, I was facing the consequences of my own choices. "Is there anything else I should know?"

"No. All I know now is that you have an indictment from the federal grand jury. I'll find out the details of the prosecution and then contact you."

When I hung up, I shared everything with Mike.

"It doesn't sound like you can do much now but wait," he said.

"Wait and pray," I added.

Calling Leesa was going to be difficult, so I waited until Mike left the store. Leesa was growing stronger every day as she faced the many problems I had caused for her, but I knew she would see this news from the lawyer as my ticket to prison. In fact, that was what I was feeling as I waited for her to answer. I was mostly upset about the pain my call would cause her and later my parents.

I did my best to explain the legal procedures, but that wasn't what she wanted to hear.

"Is the prosecutor seeking imprisonment?"

"I don't know, Lee. He probably is."

"If you go to prison, do they have any idea how long you'll be there?"

"All we know for now is that I've been indicted. The lawyer said he'll let me know when he gets more information from the prosecutor."

"I just don't know what the girls and I will do without you."

Hearing her words shook me. I felt much like I did when I first confessed my wrongdoing at the bank to her. I knew we had become stronger through the Lord and loved each other more than ever, but the thought of being separated always brought us agony. When I got off the phone, I laid my head on the counter and cried. Only the Lord could turn around the mess I had made of everything. I had to believe this or I wouldn't survive.

Only the Lord could turn around the mess I had made of everything. I had to believe this or I wouldn't survive.

I wasn't in any condition to call my parents until later in the day. When I got them on the phone, it was clear that they both were trying to encourage me.

"I know this is hard, Kevin," Mom said, "but you will make it, and so will your family." I knew she meant what she said, but I could detect worry in her voice.

After hearing the pain in Leesa's and my parents' voices, I was reminded that we never sin in isolation. All of our wrongdoings affect the ones we love and, to varying degrees, even those we don't know.

Don's comparison of the lengthy legal process to a cloud hanging over me was accurate. It stayed with me continually, even when I wasn't quite cognizant of it. Whenever I laughed with my girls or talked with Leesa about her day, I could forget the trouble I was yet to face for a few brief minutes. Then the realization would come rushing back that soon I could be separated from my family without any means to support or protect them. And for all I knew, I could be separated from them for several years. I couldn't change any of this. My wrongdoing had positioned me so that I couldn't move forward. I couldn't start a new job or even invest my life into a ministry, although I now had turned to the Lord. All I could do was wait. I expressed all of these feelings to Don over the phone as I told him about being indicted.

"Praise the Lord," Don said. "Now you can finally get through this after waiting a year and a half."

"But I'm still cornered," I said. "I can't figure out how to turn everything upright."

"You're exactly where you're supposed to be. There's no way you can figure it all out. And the Lord doesn't want you to figure it out."

"You told me a while back that a person overcomes a series of bad decisions by making a series of good decisions."

"That's right, son. The one decision you have been wrestling with is your decision to rest in the Lord and to fully submit to the process. Rather than trusting your ability to figure it all out and solve it, God wants you to see the reality of His help in this. If you were able to figure out the answer, then you would solve it without any revelation from Him."

"Blindly trusting is a hard thing to do."

"But it isn't blind trust; real faith gives the clearest vision," he said. "The more you lean into Him, the more you will see."

I saw my indictment as a deathblow. Don saw it as resurrection from death.

As I drove home that night reflecting on Don's words, I realized how opposed our views of my indictment were. I saw it as a deathblow. He saw it as resurrection from death.

After the girls were in bed, I shared with Leesa all that Don had said.

"He's right," she said. "The girls and I are with you."

"You need to be prepared for another set of news articles coming out about this," I said.

"Kev, I don't care about that; we've been through this with the civil suit," she said. "I'll face anything we need to face."

"Thanks, Lee. I couldn't have a better companion and friend than you. I don't know many women who would stick beside their husbands like you have."

She put her arms around me, and we didn't talk for a few minutes. Then she said, "I hate the thought of you being indicted, but let's view it as the first step toward getting us to the end of things."

In November, Mike went with me to visit Christ Temple Church one Sunday evening. I was impressed by this group of people who were meeting in the Veterans Memorial Field House, a multipurpose arena across the Kentucky border in Huntington, West Virginia. While they were building a new church across town, they met every Sunday at the Field House. Some of the church's members would gather at seven o'clock in the morning to set everything up for the service—chairs, tables, musical instruments, and an entire sound and lighting system. Then when the evening service ended at nine o'clock, they broke everything down and carted it all away, ready to begin the process again the next Sunday. What made their task even more challenging was cleaning up messes from public events that had been held the Saturday before—everything from discarded paper cups and greasy popcorn bags from a basketball game to elephant and horse manure from a circus.

Most important, I saw a faith among the people that I hadn't witnessed before. I truly felt the presence of the Lord among them. The individual testimonies and the message shared by Pastor Chuck Lawrence were encouraging. If Don had been with me that night, he would have said the people weren't simply struggling and coping but were seeing the resurrection and the life.

The following week, I brought Leesa and the girls with me to the evening service. As we were leaving, we met Pastor Chuck and his wife, Jamie. They were youthful and exuberant, with a graciousness that made people trust them immediately. As we talked briefly, I could tell Leesa was connecting well with both of them.

As we walked to our car, Leesa, always in touch with my feelings, asked, "Is there something you want to tell me?"

I stopped and looked back at the large brick arena. The members of the congregation were singing as they loaded chairs onto a truck. "This would be a good place for us, especially as we wait for the outcome of my case. Wouldn't it?"

"Yes," she said. "I think we need to be here."

The more we visited Christ Temple, the more convinced I was that our connection with this church would have great implications. What those were to be, I didn't know and wouldn't until years later.

My friendship with Don was unlike any relationship I had ever had. He was more to me than simply a spiritual mentor. We had become spiritually tied together, traveling on separate yet related paths. I was potentially moving toward imprisonment, which meant isolation and separation from my family. In contrast, Don was growing out of an isolated life into developing new friendships. Leaving his bare shack and moving into the high-rise was the best example of this.

I knew the value and worth of my friend, but sadly not everyone could see what I did in this man. I noticed that people were more receptive to Don after he had changed his appearance and became known as my employee. However, most people who became aware of his prior lifestyle saw him only as a man dressed in rags. Even so, Don never failed to see the value in everyone—no matter their appearance or their rudeness.

I was reminded of this false view of Don when I described him to my lawyer. I appreciated my lawyer's quiet demeanor and had begun to understand the benefit of being represented by someone who didn't incite anger from the prosecution, but he never seemed to understand about my friend.

"Don feels God's hand is on every detail of my case," I told him. "He says you and I need to pray through this."

My lawyer was civil in acknowledging the importance of doing all we could for the case, but we never prayed.

Time and time again I shared with him whatever new insight I had learned from Don. These Christian principles were helping me through my darkest hour, so I thought they were valuable to everyone. Ultimately, I received polite answers but never felt the teaching struck him in the same way.

At first I was taken aback by his response, but as I reflected on our conversations, I saw that the problem could have been my inaccurate explanation of Don. How could I convey this unique person with words? Also, I figured, my lawyer had likely seen quite a number of clients who suddenly turned to "jailhouse" religion out of fear or a desire to manipulate the system. A conversion expressed by a criminal caught in the act didn't hold much weight in the legal system.

My lawyer had likely seen a number of clients who suddenly turned to "jailhouse" religion.

My mother was a stronghold during this time, but after a while it all began to wear on her. I didn't know it until one day when I stopped by her house on my way home. I could tell by her expression that something was weighing her down.

"What's going on, Mom?"

"Have you seen much of your neighbor friends lately?"

"I've seen some of them, but not all." I named the families that I hadn't seen for months.

"So what happened with most of your friends?" she asked.

"They went in another direction after the civil suit came out in the paper."

"They're not much more than fair-weather friends, if you ask me."

"Why are you getting upset over this?" I asked. "I've told you before how some of them had moved on."

"I know," she said.

"Then what's the problem?"

"I just don't like all the bank is bringing against you," she said. "There were others involved, and they should also be paying for this."

"Mom, you're acting like I'm innocent," I said. I was surprised at her words. She didn't seem to be the same person who had frequently told me to face what I'd done. "I'm guilty. I did wrong and got caught."

"What about the others?"

"That's between them and the Lord," I said. "I made a commitment that I would be forthright about everything. This is what you've always encouraged, and that's all I can do."

"But you can't be passive, Kevin. If you are, people will beat you down."

"You have to understand that I am not the victim in this," I said. "I can't respond to the people at the bank or my unfaithful friends in the same way they're acting toward me."

"You need to be aggressive," she said. "Your babies deserve for you to fight."

I spent the next few minutes trying to convince her that her anger was misplaced, but it was useless. She just wouldn't see it my way. She acknowledged that I had done wrong, but she didn't want me to bear the full consequences, now that I was facing criminal conviction. I left her house surprised and frustrated.

"What she expressed to you yesterday was her heartfelt instinct as a mother wanting to protect her boy."

The next morning I complained to Don that my mother needed correcting. "I don't understand what she was thinking yesterday," I said. "She wants to believe I'm partially innocent in everything."

"No, son," Don said. "That's not what she's saying at all."

This wasn't the first time Don had surprised me with his perspective. "So what are you telling me, Don?"

"She knows you made mistakes and has said as much," he said. "What she expressed to you yesterday was her heartfelt instinct as a mother wanting to protect her boy."

"But she's not seeing it clearly."

"Yes she is, son. She's not moving away from everything she has said to you in the past. You just need to see beyond her words and understand her."

"Okay," I said, "but her attitude is wrong."

"It isn't a matter of her attitude," he said. "You're asking her to not be your mother."

His words disarmed me a bit, and I said, "Well, maybe you're right."

"You can't expect her to go against her natural desire to protect you," he said. "God has placed these instincts in her toward her children."

"I do understand that," I said.

Don went on to explain that the Lord has instilled a nurturing and protective spirit in both parents, but especially the mother. "Sin and guilt can quench this in people, but it's there."

"Mom and Dad have always been protective," I said. "Leesa and I feel this way about our girls."

"And your mother, your father, Leesa, and you will always feel this way."

One Saturday morning I called my lawyer and asked, as I had done several times before, if anything could be done to speed up the process. I figured he must think that I was a hard case to deal with, so I tried to approach the subject as subtly as I could.

"Just wait and let the process take its course," he said.

I knew his answer before he gave it, but I was restless that day. After I got off the phone, I couldn't concentrate and was useless the rest of the day.

That afternoon Leesa came to the store. As she swept the floor with Lindsey by her side, I moved back and forth between stocking shelves and helping Lauren dust. Every time I walked by the clock, it seemed like the hands had not moved. Leesa watched me pass her yet again and said, "Honey, what's bothering you today?"

I looked at Leesa and then turned to see what she was looking at. Several boxes lay open in the aisle, with a few canned goods stacked on the floor. I had not unpacked even one complete box, and half of the items were in the wrong spot.

I faced Leesa and said, "It's just one of those days when it seems nothing is moving forward with my case."

"It may seem that way," she said, "but it's all in the Lord's timing."

"I just want to confront everything now and get past it. Until then, we're kind of hanging."

"I know you believe what Don has told you about being in the right place."

"I do."

"You don't have to get upset," she said. "You just have to wait; there's nothing else you can do."

I looked behind Leesa and didn't see Lindsey. "Where's Lindsey?"

The bell rang at the front, and we turned to see Lindsey running out the door.

"She's outside!" Leesa dropped her broom, and we both raced out front.

Our three-year-old had cleared the parking lot and was running directly toward the busy traffic. I knew the drivers were going too fast to see her in time. With a few more steps, she would be struck by a car that was racing down the avenue at a phenomenal speed.

We both screamed, "Stop, Lindsey, stop!" and I prayed out loud, "Jesus, please spare our baby girl!"

Leesa, in her raw fear, made it past the parking lot before me. She lunged forward and grabbed Lindsey by the ruffles on her bottom. When she jerked her back, Lindsey's nose was only inches from grazing the passing car door.

The sudden turmoil upset Lindsey, and she let out a wail.

"Everything is okay," Leesa said. "You must never go outside without Mommy or Daddy."

I carried Lindsey back to the store. Inside, Leesa's legs buckled underneath her. I tried to catch her with my free arm, but she dropped to her knees.

"Honey, are you all right?"

"Yes," she said, slowly getting back up on her feet. "After being so charged up, I just felt weak."

As I watched Leesa comfort Lindsey and thank the Lord for our child, I realized that I too was shaking. It was a sobering moment, and I learned a lesson that I have never forgotten. We could have lost Lindsey—all because I allowed my impatience with the case to divert my attention from her. There was nothing I could do to change the speed of the legal process, and yet I let it completely absorb me. Watching out for the safety of our child was something I did have control over and should have been focused on. After this, I submitted to the Lord's timing for everything. I still wanted my case and the consequences to pass quickly, but I chose to hand it over to the Lord. If He wanted me to wait longer, I was now willing to accept it.

My continuing problem, however, was that I didn't know how to live out each hour without constantly thinking about the milestones up ahead. That is, until my daughter Lauren taught me a valuable lesson.

I didn't know how to live out each hour without constantly thinking about the milestones up ahead.

With Randy watching the store, Leesa, the girls, and I took a short trip to get away. The drive was several hours long, but it was relaxing, just moving down the highway with my family. I had forgotten how pleasant it was just to see some different scenery for a few days.

Lindsey slept most of the drive, but Lauren was our energetic seven-year-old who remained wide awake and impatient for us to reach our destination.

"Are we there yet?" she asked after the first hour.

"No, honey," Leesa said. "We've got a long way to go; we've just begun."

Not quite thirty miles later, Lauren asked again, "Are we almost there?"

"No," I said. "Lauren, you just asked that a half hour ago."

"How long will this take?" she asked.

"About ten more hours," Leesa said.

I looked at Lauren in the rearview mirror. This information seemed to disturb her.

"Lauren, we've made this trip before," I said. "You know it takes all day."

I thought this exchange would check Lauren's impatience for at least a few hours, but it didn't. It was hardly another thirty minutes when she asked, "Are we getting closer?"

"Yes, we're getting closer," I said.

"So how much longer?"

"A few more hours," Leesa told her.

I watched Lauren through the mirror as I drove. She wasn't enjoying the scenery outside her window. Instead, she was glancing about the car, and then at Leesa and me.

It struck me that I was seeing an example of myself. I had made a commitment to accept the Lord's schedule—just as Lauren had agreed to accept the time it would take to arrive at our destination. However, neither one of us was patient. We were focusing on what lay ahead, and we were missing the journey itself. Suddenly I had an inspiration for my daughter.

"Do you see the cows on that hill?" I asked Lauren.

"Where?" she asked.

I nodded my head to a field running alongside the highway. It was full of brown, white-faced cows grazing and lying in groups under trees.

Lauren yelled out in delight, waking up her sister.

"I'm sure there's going to be more up ahead," I said. "Why don't you and Lindsey try to count them?"

It wasn't long before we had two excited backseat sightseers who could hardly wait for their next surprise. They counted cows and horses, and even named a few before the animals disappeared from our sight. They peered down at rivers as we passed over bridges and stared up at mountains before we moved through a tunnel. Whoever was the first one to exclaim "Slugbug!" when we saw a Volkswagen Beetle won the game.

Lauren didn't ask about our arrival time again. She had become content with the journey. Both girls slept later in the trip, but when they woke up, they were ready to enjoy more sights.

Watching Lauren changed me. I saw this as an example provided by the Lord. I told Leesa that my impatience had blinded me to the point that I was missing my journey. And it had prevented me from extracting the pleasures and life lessons that could strengthen me and our marriage. My impatience had also robbed me of wisdom that I could ultimately impart to my daughters. Obviously, I needed to change.

"From here on out, I'm going to become a better sightseer."

Leesa agreed.

"I'm going to share this with Don," I said. "From here on out, I'm going to become a better sightseer."

What the Lord had shown me through my two daughters helped me see more clearly how He had chosen my lawyer. I knew that God was the One who had brought this man to me, but I had still tried to take matters into my own hands and somehow speed up the process. Once I understood God's personal regard for me and His continual provisions, I could more fully accept my lawyer's perspective. I knew I had to let him be who he was, for he was the man the Lord had provided. In fact, this lesson was similar to what Don had taught me about my mother. I would hold on to this truth even when the judge's decision in a few months was going to be a surprise not only to my lawyer but also to the prosecution.

CHAPTER

Ten

IN THE MONTHS FOLLOWING MY INDICTMENT, the prosecutor offered a number of plea agreements, but I did not consent because they included wrongs I had not committed. I made it very plain to him and my lawyer that I would own up to every one of my wrong actions. I would not, however, confess to crimes that weren't mine, even if it meant throwing away the chance of a lighter sentence. To me, taking responsibility for unsubstantiated misdeeds was a lie and could not please the Lord. Although this sort of thing appeared to be standard practice within the legal field, I resisted it because it didn't feel right. It seemed as twisted as someone living with shame and guilt about something that was not actual sin but someone else's legalistic standards.

Finally, after understanding all the charges brought against me, I knew it was right to plead guilty to one count of misapplication of funds as a bank officer. Among all the offenses spelled out by the prosecution, this was clearly the crime that I had committed. I discussed this with Leesa and my parents before I spoke with my lawyer about my decision. Everyone was in agreement that this was the proper direction.

My trial date was set for the middle of February 1999.

The day before the trial, my lawyer called the store and told me that the prosecutor was willing to drop all other charges if I pleaded guilty to the one count of misapplication of funds.

"Of course I will," I said. "This is the crime that I've been openly admitting all along."

"If you agree to this plea, I will strongly recommend probation," he said. "And the prosecutor is not objecting to this."

"Obviously, I'd rather not be separated from my family," I said, "but when I told you I'm ready to face the consequences of my wrongdoing, I meant it."

"I know that, Kevin, but plea agreements and different recommendations of judgments are how our system works."

"Okay."

My lawyer seemed pleased with my decision. "You're a great candidate to avoid prison because you've never had any prior run-ins with the law," he said. "Now, there's no guarantee, but your history and your particular crime put you in a sentencing category that equips the judge to give you probation, home confinement, or a combination of both."

When I got off the phone, I discussed everything with my friend Mike, who had dropped by the store for a visit.

"Your lawyer is right about plea agreements and probation being aspects of our legal system," Mike said. "If you get a lighter sentence, it doesn't mean you aren't facing the responsibility for your crime; you've been open about your mistakes, and the judge will decide your penalty."

"I feel this is right."

"Yes," Mike said. "I'd go for it."

When I talked with Leesa, she also agreed. "It looks like we're getting closer to coming through all of this," she said.

The next day my parents, my sister, my brother-in-law, and Mike came with Leesa and me to the federal building in Ashland, Kentucky, for my rearraignment on the revised charge. Now that the judge was informed about my plea agreement, my trial had been dismissed.

The room where we met was down the hall from the courtroom and too small to comfortably hold all of us. Leesa and I sat across a table from my lawyer, while Mike stood against the wall. My parents, sister, and brother-in-law stood within hearing range just outside the door.

Everyone waited quietly as I read over my plea agreement. When I didn't see any reference to my being a candidate for probation or home confinement, I went back over the document again.

It was clear that the agreement gave the judge full discretion to send me to prison.

"This paper doesn't mention what we discussed yesterday on the phone," I said to my lawyer.

"What do you see missing?"

"There's nothing about probation or home confinement, as we discussed."

"You'll remember I said there wasn't any guarantee of this," he said. "I will ask that you be given probation, but I can't write it down as a contract. The decision is with the judge."

Leesa had been nervous about the rearraignment, but now I could tell she was afraid. I too was thrown off by not seeing any specifics from my prior discussion.

"I understand what you're saying," I said to my lawyer, "but this is not what you told me."

"Again, I hope you get probation or home confinement, but there are no guarantees."

I too was thrown off by not seeing any specifics about probation or home confinement.

When I saw how this quick turn of my case was upsetting Leesa, I said, "I can't sign this paper."

"The judge has already dismissed the jury based on your agreement yesterday."

"The plea agreement doesn't reflect any aspect of our conversation."

"If you change your mind now, the judge will think you're toy-ing with the court," he said. "He could choose to put you in jail over this."

I knew I had to make a quick decision. Within a couple of minutes I had to walk down the hall to the courtroom and face the judge. I so much wanted Don with us, wanted to hear his perspective, but I hadn't been able to persuade him to come to the rearraignment. The courtroom with all its trappings was too intimidating for him. And I didn't have time to get him on the phone. In the end, it was up to me to choose. The next months or years could be drastically affected by what I decided.

I remembered Don telling me that people don't make bad decisions when they're calculating them calmly, but only when they're operating in the flesh. His point was that fear, anger, or any ill state could influence a person's choice. I knew as I sat across from my lawyer that I was not in a good state to make a decision.

Finally, after praying silently, I submitted to my lawyer's advice and signed the papers. He was the expert and I was the novice. The Lord had already taught me to accept and trust this man whom He had sent me. Now was my time of testing. Even though there was a problem with the communication with my lawyer, the Lord was in charge and was obviously taking me down a particular path. Where He was leading me, I did not know.

When my lawyer left the room, I turned to Leesa. "This is the right decision," I said.

She took my hand and said, "It has to be right; I don't see any other choices."

My parents, sister, and brother-in-law, who had been intently listening to my conversation, came into the room.

"I feel your lawyer should have given you more information," Dad said. He looked disturbed.

"I'll tell you, Kevin," Mike said, "he should have been more up front with you yesterday."

"I know God is closing and opening doors so that I can only go down one path," I said to everyone.

"You've admitted your wrong and have faced it openly," Mom said. "Now that you can't change things, you must trust God and move forward."

I was happy to hear my mother say this. "If we can all agree that I'm where I'm supposed to be, then I'll move forward with confidence."

"If we can all agree that I'm where I'm supposed to be, then I'll move forward with confidence."

Everyone agreed.

This was the frame of mind I was in when I faced the judge.

My rearraignment was quick and to the point. I stood with my lawyer as the judge silently read my plea agreement. Then he looked up and said to me, "I understand you worked out a deal with the prosecution."

"Yes, Your Honor."

Next he read the document aloud.

"Do you understand what you've signed?"

"Yes, Your Honor."

I was convicted on the one count of misappropriation of funds.

My lawyer made an appeal to the judge to consider probation or home incarceration due to my clean past.

The judge thanked him for his input and then set a sentencing date for three months later in the middle of May.

As I left the courtroom, I felt relief. I was now one step closer to getting through the mess that I had created. Leesa, Mike, and my entire family all expressed the same sentiment.

"Just think," I said to everyone outside the federal building, "this step is completed; I'll never have to plead guilty before a judge again."

My lawyer still believed that I was a good candidate for probation. I hoped he was correct. Being away from my family for even a month seemed unbearable. If I were single and didn't have so many people investing their love in me, the consequence of my misdeeds would affect only me. But as it stood, my crime had already turned everyone's lives upside down.

I had finally come to the place of trusting the Lord with my future—not because of any accomplishment on my part, but because of what God had taught me over the last two years. The turmoil my family had experienced and the humiliation of my sin had broken me to the point where the only thing I could lean on was the Lord.

Over the next three months, I continued managing the store and spending time with my family. During this period, it became easier for me to entertain the possibility that I would get probation, just as my lawyer suggested.

Besides, I had talked with another lawyer friend who confirmed this possibility.

"As I consider all of these details, I'm sure the judge will give you probation, house confinement at the worst," he told me.

I had the opportunity to discuss my case with other people who weren't lawyers but had different levels of exposure to the legal field. They all leaned toward my lawyer's opinion.

I knew there were no guarantees, but probation in my situation did seem to be the most likely outcome. Also, the prosecution had no objection to this kind of sentence.

So in May, as I entered the federal building with Leesa and my parents, we all were confident that the worst scenario was home incarceration.

As I stood before the bench, my lawyer told the judge that I had led an exemplary life and regretted my mistake. He added that I was a very good candidate for probation or home incarceration.

The judge turned to the prosecutor and asked if he had any objections to this request.

The prosecutor answered that no, he had no objections.

The judge then looked at me gravely and said he had never seen someone like me come through his court, as he considered my background and my crime. He paused for a moment. Then he said that nevertheless, he didn't know why, but he was going to sentence me to twelve months in prison.

Someone behind me started to cry, but I was too stunned by the judge's decision to make out who it was. I wasn't able to do anything but stare straight ahead. I felt light-headed and as if I were standing in that courtroom completely alone.

The judge said my sentence would begin the sixteenth of June, at the federal prison in Manchester, Kentucky.

When my lawyer pressed his hand on my shoulder, I followed him robot-like to my seat.

"I don't understand it, Kevin," my lawyer said in a low voice. "I just don't understand it."

Next the judge asked if there was any representation from the bank present. Two lawyers stepped up to his bench.

The judge said that he didn't know why, but he was going to sentence me to twelve months in prison.

"I'm dismissing your lawsuit with prejudice," he said. "It's time Mr. West can get some peace."

As the two men returned to their seats, it was obvious by their expressions that they were very unhappy with this decision.

"I can't believe it," my lawyer said to me. "Do you know what just happened?" When I didn't answer, he explained, "The judge has done away with the entire civil lawsuit. It's gone forever. All you have to do now is serve your time."

"Serve my time?" I said. "I came in here believing I wasn't going to be separated from my family."

"I'm sorry, Kevin. I don't understand your sentence either."

As people were leaving the courtroom, the prosecutor came over to my lawyer.

"What was that?" he asked, referring to the judge's decision to send me to prison.

"I have no idea," my lawyer said.

I could tell that Leesa and my parents were shocked and devastated by the judgment as we walked in silence down the hallway.

"Everything is going to be all right," I said.

A news reporter hurriedly stepped into the elevator with us just before the doors closed.

"Do you care to make any kind of comment, Mr. West?"

"No," I said. I knew that the Lord had to remain my advocate, especially then, when I was feeling so down and out.

"Could you tell me if you were surprised by the judge's decision?"

"No comment," I said.

When we reached the main floor, my family and I walked quickly toward the exit. Just as we left the building, I heard the reporter make another attempt, asking, "How do you feel about the judge dismissing your civil suit?"

Leesa has always been intuitive, knowing when I can't talk and need to quietly reflect. She immediately recognized that our drive home was one of those times. I was deep in thought, as I recalled everything that had transpired to bring me to this particular place. I mean everything—good and bad, mistakes made in ignorance and those made on purpose. I thought about the solid character of my parents and the unending devotion of my wife. By the time we pulled into our driveway and parked, I felt better.

"I don't know how everything is going to play out, Lee," I said, "but the Lord is going to be our stronghold."

"I know He is," she said. "What will happen next?"

"I don't really know. I'll have to talk to my lawyer."

"We only have four weeks before you leave," she said.

I put my arm around her and pulled her closer to me. All we could do at that moment was hold each other and cry.

"One burden you don't have to carry is worrying about me and our girls," she said, wiping her eyes. "We're going to be okay."

I knew she was right. Leesa had faced this catastrophe—which I had brought upon us—and was coming through it as a stronger person. If she hadn't, I couldn't have made it. I often had the frightening sensation of frantically grabbing at jagged rock as I slipped faster down into a black crevice. During those terrifying moments, Leesa's love and faithfulness were the harness and rope that arrested my fall.

That same afternoon, I returned to the store. Randy stayed a couple of hours with me. He had heard the details about my sentence through my mother.

"Kevin, I'll make sure Leesa and the girls will be all right," he said. "My wife and I both will make sure of that."

"I really appreciate you, Randy. You're a great cousin and a wonderful friend."

"We're family, Kevin."

"We sure are." I looked at the bell perched at the entrance and thought about that bright morning in March two years earlier when Don first came through that door, how he had reached up and stopped the clapper with his fingers. "I guess I'll have to do something about my grocery store."

"We'll work something out," Randy said. "I'll run it in the evenings while Don does all the delivering. It's just a matter of finding somebody to watch it during the day."

"No," I said. "I'm going to have to sell it."

"Are you sure? Don't you want to try to figure out how you can keep it?"

"No, Randy. It makes more sense to let it go."

"That's a shame," he said. "I know it's got to be hard for you to leave it."

"Yes," I said, but he couldn't fathom just how hard it was for me to lose this place. It was much more than a small business to make ends meet. It had become a gathering spot to develop friendships with people whom I otherwise never would have known. And it was a school where I had learned so much about my customers—the brokenhearted, the abandoned, even the insecure who hid behind their own brand of braggadocio. It was also a church where I fellowshipped with believers and where I could minister to those who had an open heart to listen. But most important to me, it was the place where I'd met Don. Here in this small and modest corner grocery,

God had fostered our friendship in the most peculiar way and had transformed both of our lives.

God had fostered our friendship in the most peculiar way and had transformed both of our lives.

After Randy left, I got a call from Don.

"I heard about your sentence on the news," he said.

We spoke just briefly, and a few minutes later, I heard Don's car rumbling up onto his usual spot on the sidewalk. When he came in, he sat in front of the ice cream freezer and said, "The separation from your family will be hard, but you can't look at this as a punishment."

"Never let your life's experiences shape how you see God."

"But it is a punishment," I said, "for my crime."

"It is indeed," he said, "but I'm referring to your relationship with God."

"Yes, of course," I said. "I know the Lord has taken my mistakes and is working everything together to restore my life."

"Even more so, you need to see this direction, even to prison, as your assignment," he said. "Wherever your choices have brought you, remember that God never changes and His feelings toward you always remain the same."

"I have to admit that I was surprised by the sentence," I said. "After hearing my lawyer's perspective, as well as others', I wasn't expecting to go to prison at all."

"Even though the outcome didn't turn out as you thought, God didn't change, and the circumstances didn't change Him," he said. "Never let your life's experiences shape how you see God."

Don's words confirmed what I was finally beginning to understand, not just with my mind but with my heart. My trials had opened my eyes to see more clearly how God was arranging my path. My repentance and my resignation from the bank two years earlier weren't enough to bring me to a particular destination. The Lord, in His wisdom, wanted me to learn much on this journey through my relationships with Leesa, my girls, my parents, my sister, Randy, and many friends. And God was orchestrating everything. When I turned to the Lord for help, my growth journey had begun, but I wasn't ready to accept imprisonment until I learned to let Leesa grow through her fears and to allow my parents and friends to encourage me. I had to submit to God's timing and draw sustenance from what He taught me each day as I traveled this road. Without Don, I would have missed everything, because he was the one who had helped me see Christ through it all. One of the most life-changing revelations was that nothing could limit the Lord's ability to restore my life. He could turn even my worst decisions into opportunities, changing them from roadblocks into tunnels—whatever He desired—to carry me forward.

CHAPTER Eleven

Having only four weeks before my imprisonment left me little time to arrange everything for my departure. It was challenging enough to plan for a one-week vacation; preparing to leave my family on their own for an entire year was overwhelming. I knew I had to do everything possible to make my absence easier for Leesa and the girls. Family and good friends would keep close watch on them while I was gone, but right now I had to take care of everything I could. Most of all, I didn't want to haphazardly fritter my hours away and, in so doing, lose time being with my family.

In this state of mind, I found myself weighing every action. I constantly asked myself if this or that task was vital for the survival of my family or if it was robbing me of moments with them. At first I felt this preoccupation was wise, but it soon seized so much of my thoughts that I was emotionally and physically drained.

As always, it helped to talk things over with Don.

"How do I know which tasks should go by the wayside?" I asked. "This is much different from preparing for a short business trip."

"It is different, son, but not as different as you might think," he said.

"I have to plan."

"Yes, you have to plan, but don't worry about what is to happen in the future or you will lose what you can enjoy now."

"I'm not worrying the way I was about the future," I said. "I'm ready to serve my time. My sin sent me down the wrong path, but the Lord has set me on another."

"Worrying is borrowing from tomorrow, and it will rob you of your family today."

"I know you're ready for prison," he said, "but the future you're worrying about is the future of your family."

"Isn't this a legitimate concern?"

"It is, son, but you're not going to be here to care for them. That's why you have to entrust them to the Lord. Worrying is borrowing from tomorrow, and it will rob you of your family today."

"So it comes back to me deciding which tasks are investing into my family and which tasks are robbing them."

"First, engage with your family and don't worry about what's up ahead, because no one knows the future," he said. "Throughout these four weeks, know that the Lord is guiding your steps and then choose to do the essential tasks."

"Essential as opposed to frivolous," I said.

"Hebrews in the Living Word speaks of a curious thing," Don said. "Just as God rested on the seventh day from His works, we through faith are to enter that same rest."

"I remember reading that," I said. "How do you interpret it?"

"The work of Christ is complete. That's why He sat down on the right hand of God the Father after He purged our sins. Everything is done. We cannot add to or take away from it. When we struggle in our own efforts, we're actually trying to live life separately from the Lord. It's just like Adam believing that he could make it on his own."

"Surely God wants us to be active."

"Yes. Resting in the Lord doesn't mean doing nothing. When you rest in the Lord, you abandon your own frail attempts to live and allow the Lord to live through you. You cease from your own works just as God did after He created the universe."

"How does this play out as far as making decisions?"

"You'll understand more as you experience this," he said. "The works you abandon are worry and fear and the exhausting struggle to figure everything out. The more you trust God, the more you will rest in Him, knowing He is actively guiding you in everything, great and small."

This truth struck me more than anything Don had taught me in the past two years. I don't think I could have fully appreciated this teaching if it hadn't been for everything Don had shared with me along the way. It felt as if all his prior words had been leading up to this point. This was the best explanation of trusting God with every aspect of one's life that I had ever heard.

> "The works you abandon are worry and fear and the exhausting struggle to figure everything out."

Don took my hand and prayed, "Lord, teach us how to rest in You so that Your voice becomes clearer to us, just as the shepherd's call is to his sheep."

Don was right. The more I rested in the Lord, the more I could sense Him guiding me. I was free from anguishing over which tasks were important and which should be abandoned. My mind was clearer and, surprisingly, this freedom energized me. I was still burdened over being separated from my family, but as I leaned more into the Lord with a childlike faith, I was more convinced that He would plant each of my steps.

I DECIDED TO KEEP the corner grocery building but sell the business. The rent would be just enough to continue the payments on the building. It didn't take long before I found a woman who was interested and ready to take over the store. After we worked out the details, she allowed me the time I needed to clear out the stock she didn't want.

Soon after receiving my sentence, I made personal contact with Pastor Chuck Lawrence at Christ Temple, asking him to make sure that my family would never feel unwelcome at his church. I did this because Leesa and the girls needed the encouragement of a church, in addition to the support I knew they would receive from family and friends. Pastor Chuck said he was more than happy to do so. Leesa and I had gotten to know him and his wife, Jamie, over the prior six months, so they knew of my crime and potential imprisonment.

Since it was already May, I made arrangements with a high-school boy to cut our grass, rake our leaves in the fall, and shovel our sidewalks if we had a harsh winter snow. I checked our cars, making certain that all the fluid levels and the air pressure in the tires were right. I even filled the tanks with gas, knowing I wouldn't be there to do any of this again for a long time. And I double-checked our insurance policies and bills to make certain everything was up-to-date.

Between taking care of the many details of living, I made a deliberate effort to enjoy my family. As I learned to rest in the Lord as Don suggested, I was able to savor wonderful moments laughing with my family and looking ahead to when I would return to them. Our whole family—including my parents and sister—was committed to being positive and only focusing on do-able preparations and, as Don had suggested, "taking care of the day-to-day matters."

As Leesa saw how determined I was to not let our last four weeks be stolen by worrying over the future, she became stronger. She began seeing our situation as one of life's passageways. And the more she saw it this way, the more it helped me to see it as well.

Leesa began seeing our situation as one of life's passageways.

My walk with Christ thrived during this period. My relationship with my wife and children was better than it had ever been. Without realizing it, I became a more loving husband and attentive father. I had always adored Leesa and my daughters, and I had loved my parents and sister, but now it seemed these feelings rose up inside of me at every turn. I knew this was the Spirit of God working through me as I rested in the Lord.

The most difficult task during this time was trying to explain to Lauren and Lindsey why I would be gone for such a long time. Months earlier, Leesa and I had told the girls that I had done something wrong at the bank and couldn't work there anymore. Their understanding of how a bank functioned was very basic, and it was impossible to convey to their young minds how wrong my crime had been. However, I wanted them to know the truth. To compare my misdeed to one of their friends stealing Lauren's or Lindsey's doll would not have been accurate. Instead, I told them my mistake was like someone taking the doll not to keep but to let other friends play with it.

"Why do that?" Lauren asked.

"That person would benefit by making more friends," I said. "The bad part is the doll wasn't theirs to take."

In the end they really only understood that I had done something wrong.

As my prison time drew near, Leesa and I didn't try to explain my crime again. Instead, we tried to prepare them for my upcoming absence.

"It's like when you girls do something you're not supposed to and you have to sit awhile in your room," Leesa said.

"How long will you have to be in your room?" Lindsey asked.

"Well, sweetheart," I said, "your daddy won't sit in his room, but will have to go somewhere else for a while."

"Where?" Lauren asked.

"I have to stay at another place in Kentucky."

"For how long?" she asked, her eyes tearing up.

It was so upsetting to see her cry that I couldn't answer her without my voice cracking.

Leesa stepped in and answered, "He has to be gone for one year, but we're going to visit and write to your daddy."

Lauren jumped on my lap and hung on to the front of my shirt, crying, "I don't want you to go."

Lindsey started bawling, so Leesa picked her up and moved over beside me on the couch. After letting them both cry for a few minutes, Leesa said, "Girls, everything is going to be all right."

"We are still going to see each other," I said.

"When?" Lauren asked.

"We're going to see Daddy every Saturday," Leesa said.

Lauren looked at her mother and then back at me.

"That's right, honey," I said. "We'll see each other every Saturday."

"And then you'll be coming back home again?"

"Yes, he will after a while," Leesa said.

This seemed to satisfy Lauren, at least for the moment. Once she accepted it, Lindsey was better too. I well knew it was going to be a very hard year for both of them, and this just tore my heart out.

While Leesa was busy with the girls, I left the house to talk privately with my parents. As always, they knew before we even walked back to the den that I had something very important to share with them. We all sat in the same seats as when I had first told them about my wrongdoing at the bank.

"I know you both will keep a watch over Leesa and our girls," I said, "but can you make a special effort to look after them?"

"You don't have to worry about this," Dad said. "We will take care of them."

"Of course we will," Mom said.

"You both know how Leesa is; it's not in her nature to ask for anything."

"We know Leesa and love her dearly," Mom said. "And those two baby angels mean everything to us."

"Always come out and just ask Leesa what she needs," I said. "If she hedges, push a little more to find out what it is."

"We will," Mom said.

I knew I didn't have to make this request, but just hearing their answer encouraged me.

With three weeks left before my departure, I initiated the summer months for my daughters by opening our swimming pool. I made certain the heater and the pump were both working. Then I cleaned out the few leaves that had somehow fallen into the water despite it being covered through the fall and winter months. As I tested the pH and chlorine levels, I thought how this was one of many duties that would soon become Leesa's responsibility. Preparing the pool for summer was important so she and the girls could continue in their same routine even during my absence.

Another important task was clearing out the garage. I always did this at the beginning of every summer. This particular job was especially difficult now because every item that I picked up or shifted reminded me of places we had gone or moments we had enjoyed as a family. It was the same as glancing through a family photo album. A striped inflatable ball faded by several summers at the beach, a picnic basket split down one corner from carrying food and Lauren's favorite dolls, a snow shovel with one corner bent because I was hurriedly digging through a surprise snow to make it to work—it seemed that everything I touched had its own story to tell. What kept me from sinking into a sad state was remembering to rest in the Lord. I was moving ahead into a specific assignment and would return the following year to build more memories with my family.

What kept me from sinking into a sad state was remembering to rest in the Lord.

It didn't take long before Lauren and Lindsey heard me banging around the garage and came inside to help. Showing them how to stack their piles and where to sweep took up most of my time, but I savored every minute with them. As with me, everything they saw and touched reminded them of times with the family. We spent the rest of the afternoon together, recalling funny moments and laughing. It was one of those precious times that I wouldn't trade for anything.

RANDY CAME BY THE STORE to help me gather the stock that the new owner couldn't use as well as a number of my personal belongings. He worked at his usual fast pace, pulling cans off the shelf and packing them neatly into boxes, never taking a break.

"Randy, you've been an incredible help to me over the last two years."

"I'm glad to do it, Kevin."

"People are going to miss your gifts of sodas and coffee, not to mention the hundreds of suckers you've thrown to kids."

He laughed and sat down on one of the boxes. Then his face turned somber. "I'm sure going to miss you, Cousin."

"I'll miss you too," I said. "We've had some life-changing discussions in this place."

"Yes, we have." He lifted his cap and ran his hand back through his hair. "We've had some real Spirit-filled revivals."

"Well, the rent from the new owner will help me keep the building," I said, "but I'm still trying to figure out how to take care of our house payments."

"I've wanted to talk to you about that." Randy paused and then said, "I'm going to take care of it for you."

"What do you mean, Randy? I can't ask you to do that."

"You haven't asked me to do anything," he said. "I'm going to take care of it."

"How can you, with the responsibilities you've got with your own bills?"

"Just like you said—I'm still trying to figure it out." He pointed his finger at me. "You can rest assured that your house payments will be made every month."

I was so bowled over by his commitment to me and my family that I actually stumbled over my words to thank him. If my cousin said he'd do something, he would do it. His word was his bond. I knew then and there that I no longer had to worry about preserving our home.

As June approached and my time to leave was drawing closer, Leesa and I spent a lot of time holding each other, sometimes crying about our upcoming separation, but also laughing as we recalled our cherished moments together. Years earlier, when she and I had exchanged marriage vows, I could never have comprehended how much my love for her would grow. Our sadness over being apart from each other didn't weaken our conviction that the Lord was in total control and that it was right for me to face the penalty of my deeds. Knowing that Leesa loved me unconditionally and would be here upon my return heightened my commitment to follow God, no matter where I was.

During my last week as I was sweeping the store, I heard the rumbling of a car and the familiar double jingle of the entrance bell. I dropped my broom and hurried down the aisle to greet my friend.

When Don saw me, he stopped at the counter. "Hello, son."

"I'm glad you came in, Don." He looked better than ever, dressed in khaki pants and a new white button-down shirt. He had just trimmed his beard and cut his hair. It was getting harder to remember that long-haired man who once came into my store wearing tattered trousers and a soiled shirt. The truth was that he was not the same man he'd been. And neither was I.

The truth was that he was not the same man he'd been. And neither was I.

"I see you're getting everything ready to move on to the next phase of your journey," he said.

"That's right. This is my last day at the store."

"The store will be here when you get back," he said, "so maybe it won't be your last day."

"That's true."

As I stood there looking at Don, I wondered if my efforts never to embarrass him with invasive questions or pointed comments might have stifled my expression of appreciation toward him. Telling him that God had used him to preserve me and my family would not have been an exaggeration. For a moment I felt panicked, not knowing how I was going to make it in prison without his continuing presence in my life.

I felt panicked, not knowing how I was going to make it in prison without Don's continuing presence in my life.

Don apparently saw the sudden shift of emotions in my face. He looked intently at me and asked, "What is it, son?"

I tried to explain all that was running through my mind and everything I was feeling, but my words didn't come near to conveying my love for him. "I'm going to miss you, my good friend," I said, struggling to hold back my tears.

"I'll miss you, son," he said. "But we will write to each other, and God will bring our paths together again."

I knew he was right. I would continue our friendship throughout and beyond my imprisonment.

We talked about first meeting two years and three months earlier, reflecting on the many changes in both of our lives. It was the first time he expressed how happy he was living in the high-rise.

"I've really found many good friends there," he said.

"And what about Velma?" I asked with a smile.

"You know, son, how I've always just loved her voice." He looked about the room as he thought about my question. "That wonderful lady is the best friend I have there."

There was more sweeping to do, but I decided to lock up and walk out with my friend. We carried some boxes to my car, and then stood awhile outside, enjoying the sunny day. Don wanted to make sure everyone in my family was doing well, as I was about to leave them. He was also concerned about my parents, my sister, and even Randy.

"I think everyone is doing fine," I said.

"And you?"

I told him imprisonment was the consequence for my sin, but I knew God was turning it all in a direction for His purpose. "The Lord has brought me too far to just let the bottom drop out," I said.

"That's right. The Lord is taking you on an assignment down there. You may plan your way, but the Lord is directing your steps." He smiled as he talked about God's hand on me. "Just remember, whether you find yourself in a good or a not-so-good place, it doesn't change what's inside of you."

"Whether you find yourself in a good or a not-so-good place, it doesn't change what's inside of you."

"I'll remember," I said.

"Lord, let Kevin feel You holding his right hand and hear Your words to not fear," Don prayed.

We hugged each other and cried.

"I'll be here when you come back." Don took off his glasses and wiped his eyes. "I'll write you, son."

I got in my car and started the engine, but then turned it off. I looked out the window and watched my dear friend climb into his old red Buick. I had to chuckle to myself when I thought of how he had parked in that very place on the sidewalk the first day he came into the store, and how that space had become his reserved spot. He gunned his engine several times to keep it running and waved at me.

I knew we would keep in touch through letters during my imprisonment because we had become the kind of friends described in Proverbs, who stick closer than brothers. What I didn't know on that warm day in June as I waved back and watched him drive away was the sad truth that I was never going to see him again.

CHAPTER

Twelve

THE DAY FINALLY ARRIVED for me to go to prison. I woke up just as the sun was rising and looked over at Leesa. She was already awake.

"Well, this is the day," I said.

"Yes, it is."

It was obvious as we got ready that Leesa was trying to keep that morning as upbeat as possible with her usual hug and bright voice. I struggled to do the same, but it was difficult. I felt like wrapping my arms around her and the girls and never letting them go. I still knew I was on course with my destination, but it didn't rid me of the anguish and pain of leaving my family.

"I guess I'd better wake up Lauren and Lindsey," Leesa said.

I put my arms around her, and we both broke down and cried.

"We're going to make it, honey," Leesa said.

"I just adore you and our girls," I said. "I sure was a lucky boy when you first said yes to that Christmas party."

"Well, I had to think about it," she joked. "I didn't like boys who stood me up."

"I never did it again."

As we stood together in our bedroom, newly awash with sunlight, I knew I was holding God's great gift to me. I was married to a woman who magically became more beautiful with each year, who loved me and our daughters more than herself. She had forgiven my deeds that had thrown her headlong into financial turmoil and public humiliation, with no thought of ever leaving my side. I knew the Lord had joined us together in that mysterious union described in Genesis when a man and woman become one flesh. She, indeed, was my other half, and I was hers.

I didn't want my family to watch my departure, so Leesa agreed to take the girls to my parents' before I left. I had already said my good-byes to Mom, Dad, and my sister the day before.

When the girls first got up, they were still groggy with sleep. It wasn't until Lauren was bathed and dressed that it fully dawned on her that her daddy was finally leaving. She ran to me, fiercely grabbing hold of my sleeves and wailing. Naturally, this set off Lindsey as well.

Leesa saw how this was tearing me apart and intervened.

"Girls, we talked about this. Everything is going to be all right. We're going to write Daddy and see him every Saturday."

When Lauren slowly released my sleeves, I knelt down and drew both girls closer. They smelled fresh and clean—their hair still damp from their baths. "Right now I'm holding the sweetest girls in the whole world."

Lauren turned her face up to me and said, "And we're going to see you every Saturday."

"That's right," I said. "Every Saturday."

After kissing the girls and putting them in the car, I walked around to the driver's side to Leesa. I reached through the window and kissed her.

"Kev, don't worry about us," she said. "You've done everything possible to prepare us, and we have a great number of family and friends to support us."

"I know."

"We'll trust God that this will be shorter than a year."

We kissed again and I said, "I love you."

All I can do at this juncture is trust the Lord and submit to the process.

"I know," she said, "and I love you."

With those last words, she backed up the car and drove away. I watched until she was out of sight. I felt helpless, knowing I couldn't change anything. I couldn't alter yesterday or even make the previous hour better or worse. It was clear to me how sin always brings consequences. *All I can do at this juncture,* I thought, *is trust the Lord and submit to the process.*

Tim, the husband of my lawyer friend Mary, had offered weeks earlier to drive me to Manchester, Kentucky, where I was to serve my time. He arrived at nine o'clock sharp, and we started out on the three-hour trip together. He was a kind man who reminded me a lot of my father. He never wasted his words on frivolous topics, but only discussed important issues at hand. That morning as we traveled the 150 miles southward, we talked very little. I was certain Tim was being especially sensitive, leaving me alone with my thoughts about Leesa and the girls.

The only conversation I remember having with him that day as we passed miles of fields and trees, green with new summer, was when I thanked him for his friendship. "You and Mary have been so good to me," I said.

"We're glad to support you, Kevin," he answered.

After we arrived at the correctional facility, Tim said, "Mary and I are going to keep in touch with Leesa and the girls while you're gone."

"Thank you, Tim."

THE PRISON COMPRISED several buildings set in a circle with the administrative offices at the entrance. The massive block-shaped architecture appeared misplaced amidst fields and sloping hills, thick with trees and wild growth. I figured they'd had to dynamite this area and grade hundreds of acres before it was flat enough for construction.

Even though I was prepared to begin my time, I was crushed when Tim drove away. After he was gone, I truly felt alone. I was now officially separated from family and friends. I didn't know anyone, and no one knew me. I was less than 200 miles from home, but it seemed as far away as the moon. I had never yearned for a familiar face as much as I did at that moment. I would have welcomed anyone who shared some kind of history with me. This empty feeling eventually gave me insight into why all the prisoners wanted to know where I was from. If they could find someone who knew their family or who went to their school or even had walked the streets of their town, they could find solace knowing they were still connected to the outside.

The warden and other administrators made certain that I understood the layout of the facility, my specific schedule, the rules of conduct, and the consequences of resisting authority. I was shown where I was to sleep, eat, and work for the next twelve months. At the end of my orientation, I had to exchange my clothes for a white shirt, white trousers, and a pair of brown boots.

"Report to the kitchen tomorrow directly after breakfast," the warden said.

My work in the kitchen kept me busy after each meal. I wiped off dishes and stacked them on a conveyor belt that continually carried them, along with cups and eating utensils, into a massive washing machine. I swept the floors, wiped down counters, and cleaned the large pots and fryers after every meal. I was glad to fill my days doing something productive. Working with my hands freed my mind so I could reflect upon the scriptures I had memorized during the past couple of years. It also gave me time to think about Leesa and my girls and to pray for them. I never knew what each one was doing during those moments, so I just asked God to comfort them.

Another inmate helping in the kitchen was Benny, a really likable twenty-three-year-old black man. Standing a good head taller than most of the prisoners, he weighed more than 230 pounds, every bit of it muscle. Most people were intimidated by his size, until they saw his infectious smile or heard him joking with another inmate. Then it was obvious that he was just a big playful kid.

I felt a heavy burden for Benny. His brother was a drug pusher who had been killed during one of his deals. After his murder, Benny took over his illegal operation with the intention of supporting his mother. Ever since he had been convicted and received a six-year sentence, he was constantly haunted by what his mother thought of him. Despite Benny's regrets, I was concerned that he might continue down that same dark road, unless, of course, he could meet the true person of Christ.

I was concerned that Benny might continue down that same dark road, unless, of course, he could meet the true person of Christ.

"Your mother never suspected that you were making money from drugs?" I asked one afternoon as we were cleaning up after lunch.

"No way." He stopped wiping the counter and stared across the room, deep in thought. "After I got caught, she kept saying, 'My Benny wouldn't do this.'" He shook his head and looked at me. "When nobody else cares, your mother keeps believing in you. I wonder all the time what she's thinking now."

Benny always appeared jovial and ready for a hearty laugh, but every time I heard him speak of his mother, he was somber and often sad.

I enjoyed my time with Benny, but his work ethic left much to be desired. One time I caught him sweeping the center of the floor, neglecting the area underneath the tables.

"Benny, why not do a better job and clean the whole floor?" I asked.

"Sure," he said. He swept the crumbs and debris up against the baseboard and then rested on a milk crate.

Sometimes he would dry an entire pot; other times he'd slap the bottom with a towel and say, "Good enough."

I never took offense at his ways. I really just wanted him to develop habits that could help him on the outside. If he could do his best with small jobs, I'd tell him, then he'd be prepared to handle the bigger jobs.

"Where are those bigger jobs?" he asked, laughing.

"I'll tell you, Benny, they come to those who are ready for them." I told him the parable about the two servants who wisely invested and increased their master's talents. "Because of their faithfulness, they were put in charge of many more things."

"Ah, come on, man," he said. "Where's that in the Bible?"

"The twenty-fifth chapter of Matthew."

He wasn't satisfied until he went back to his room and read it for himself. The next morning, the first thing he said to me was, "Kevin, that story is really in there."

I had to laugh at his surprise.

"You were right about those two servants, but you didn't tell me about the third guy," Benny said. "That dude didn't use his talents and lost it all."

This was the beginning of our spiritual talks.

A FEW DAYS AFTER COMING TO PRISON, I got involved in an evening Bible study meeting with two other inmates. None of us ever discussed the crimes that brought us to Manchester. It was a matter of inmate ethics never to ask. Sometimes I would overhear someone discussing his past, but mostly the topic was never approached unless, as in Benny's case, someone wanted to offer the information. The two men in the Bible study group could have been drug pushers, thieves, or the perpetrators of a number of crimes, but it didn't matter. We all focused on Christ and the new life we sought through Him.

> **I found myself sharing what Don had taught me and describing my struggle in finally living out these life-changing truths.**

Invariably, the scriptural topics led to each of us talking about his loved ones. I had never intended to lead the Bible study group or any of the discussions, but it happened anyway. It was a natural progression for me to accept this role, because I hurt for these men and understood their fears and guilt. I found myself not only sharing what Don had taught me, but also describing my pain and struggle in finally living out these life-changing truths.

One man was haunted by most everything he read in the Scriptures. Every passage reminded him of his crime and weighed him down. It became easier for him to keep his Bible closed and avoid what he felt was confrontation.

"You're not seeing the finished work of Christ," I said to him. "Once you understand who you are in Him, the Scriptures won't put a burden on you, but will release you from your burden."

He had never heard this before. After a few weeks, he finally came to see that he was forgiven, that Jesus had purged his sins, and that Jesus now sat at the right hand of the Father interceding on our behalf—all proof of the finished work of Christ. After this change, the man could hardly put down the Bible. Overwhelmed by the many spiritual treasures he discovered, he was compelled by compassion to share them with others.

The other man in our study group was angry at his wife, who he said was cold and unforgiving.

"I know I've done wrong and caused her a lot of grief," he said, "but I'm the one having to pay the price, and I got over it."

"She's paying the price also," I said. "Everybody in here is a son or a husband or a father to somebody. We can't commit wrong deeds without our choices affecting someone."

"I know she's having a hard time because of me, but don't you think she should get over it after a year?"

"Maybe not," I said. "You can't expect her to process this experience as quickly or in the same way you do. She's a different person."

"You're right about her being different," he said sarcastically.

"I realized that my imprisonment is harder on my family than it is on me," I said.

"Why would it be?"

"You know what you're facing each day and probably feel like you can handle it," I said. "But not your family. They can only see it as if from a distant window. They're not here with you seeing everything firsthand, so their imaginations can exaggerate what they think you're going through day after day."

That was the only time he and I discussed his wife, but I'm convinced he took my words to heart. The change in him wasn't quick or even dramatic. Over the next couple of months, however, the man's permanent frown and caustic tone slowly dissipated. When his wife visited on Saturdays, the conversations appeared sweeter and were no longer filled with the usual arguments.

Over the next couple of months, the man's permanent frown and caustic tone slowly dissipated.

One man with the unusual nickname Turbo never joined our Bible study group, but I still had many opportunities to talk with him. He was thin and lanky, his face hard and empty of emotion. He always claimed that he didn't care about his children. "My wife left me and decided to keep those kids," he said. "So there's nothing I can do for her or them."

"Don't you miss your children?" I asked.

Don kept his word and wrote to me. A letter from him arrived every two weeks.

"I don't know" was always his answer. This told me that he did miss them, but something in his past inhibited him from admitting it. I thought of Don's story, the one he told me at the hamburger shop, about the man with the blue bandana who had lost his child. Turbo's life had most likely been ruptured in the same way. His guilt was like handcuffs preventing him from reaching out to his children.

DON KEPT HIS WORD and wrote to me. A letter from him arrived every two weeks. The handwriting was messy, and the sentences slanted wildly up or down the page, but his notes were priceless. I could hear Don's voice in each of them, as he encouraged me to look to the end of my imprisonment when I would be reunited with my family.

I answered each letter, writing him about all that was happening with me and the other inmates.

The most precious letters came from Leesa. I cherished every familiar phrase or word that reflected her sweetness. The most encouraging subjects she covered might not have been world-changing to others, but they helped me survive the separation from her and my girls. I savored every story about Lauren and Lindsey swimming in the pool or playing in the yard. I could never hear enough about her time spent with Mom and Dad. Most of all, I drank in all her affectionate comments that reaffirmed her love for me.

Lauren sent me cards made in school or church with "I love you, Daddy" printed in large letters. Lindsey's writing was harder to read, but I adored those loose, scraggly lines spilling across blue construction paper that attempted to say, "I miss you, Daddy."

I also got letters from my parents, sister, and friends from church. Pastor Chuck Lawrence and his wife, Jamie, sent me cards. Every evening after dinner as I stood with other inmates at mail call, I anticipated the wonderful treasures that awaited me in each envelope.

As much as I found encouragement through the many letters, nothing compared to seeing my family face-to-face every Saturday. It was difficult waiting those six days for the time I could kiss Leesa and hold my babies. Mom came as well. My sister and brother-in-law couldn't come every Saturday, but they were such a blessing when they did arrive. Even some friends visited, but they were careful not to take away my time with family. My father, however, just couldn't bear seeing me in prison and never came. I couldn't understand this at first, because he had always been and still is one of the strongest, most steadfast individuals I have ever known. Finally I accepted that it was a matter of allowing my father, in his own way, to process his agony over my incarceration. This was what Don had taught me to do with Leesa and my mother, and this is what I was passing on to other inmates. In the long run, my father ministered to me in a deeply personal way through his letters. He wasn't verbose or fancy with words, but he knew how to communicate affection to his son.

On the day of visitation, I'd wait along with the other inmates to be called. Once I heard my name, I'd come to a holding area where an officer read the list of my visitors, making certain that every adult had had a background check. If everything was in order, another officer patted me down, feeling the full area of my limbs and torso, checking for foreign objects, notes, or anything that I might illegally pass to an outsider.

Every time I walked out into the spacious visiting room, I was lovingly mobbed by Lauren and Lindsey, both fighting to sit in my lap.

On the second Saturday of my incarceration, the girls were pulling aggressively at my shirt.

"Pick me up, Daddy!" Lindsey cried. "Pick me up!"

"Okay, honey," I said, lifting her. "Now let me give your mommy a kiss."

Leesa laughed and leaned over to kiss me. "I guess I'd better start running faster, so I don't get beat out of a kiss."

Lindsey locked her arms around my neck with her face pressed against mine. "Now give Daddy a chance to find a place for us to sit," I said, trying to spot an empty table away from the other inmates also visiting with their families.

"Here, sweetie," my mother said, holding out her arms to Lindsey, "let your Maw Maw carry you till we find some chairs."

"No," Lindsey said, gripping me harder.

"Girls, how about just us three taking a walk outside into the compound?" I said, thinking it might be a good way to relax Lindsey. "I've got something to show you."

They both agreed, but Lindsey wanted to be carried. We went outside to the center of the correctional facility where all the walkways led to various buildings. I walked as far as I was allowed and pointed toward the kitchen.

"That building down there is where your daddy works," I said.

"What do you do in there?" Lauren asked.

"I help wash the dishes," I said. "I sweep the floors, and I clean all the pots and pans for the next meal."

Lauren stared at the building with interest.

Lindsey couldn't have cared less. She was too busy making certain that I didn't escape from her grip.

Finally Lindsey relaxed her hold on me, and I tried to set her down. She started crying, so I lifted her up again.

"Let's go back and see your mommy and Maw Maw," I said.

"Have the girls been good?" I asked Leesa and Mom after we all sat down at a corner table.

Before either could answer, Lauren spoke up, saying, "Not really."

"What do you mean?" I asked.

"Lindsey splashed water on Mommy when she was walking along the pool."

"I'm sure it was an accident."

"No, it wasn't," Lauren said. "She did it on purpose."

Leesa gave me a wink, and I said, "Well, maybe your mother needed to get wet."

When the girls both laughed, my mother thoughtfully took the moment to pick up Lindsey.

"I'm going to take a short walk outside with Mommy," I said. When Lindsey objected, I added, "We three had a nice walk together, and now I need to show Mommy everything I showed you."

Lindsey reluctantly agreed to stay inside, and I walked out into the compound with Leesa.

"What's going on?" I asked. "Lindsey's having an unusually hard time today."

"She'll be all right," she said. "She just misses you."

"Now tell me how you're doing. I know it's got to be hard at times." I could see the stress in Leesa's face when I said these words. But she tried to lift my burden by evading discussions about her struggles and only talking about positive subjects.

"I just miss you, honey. We all miss you."

"I miss you too, and think about you and the girls every hour of the day," I said. "Lee, I feel like there's something bothering you that you're not telling me."

"I don't want you to worry about anything," she persisted.

"What is it, Lee?"

She shook her head and said, "They didn't renew my contract at Oakview."

"What?" I was dumbfounded. "Why not?"

"The funding this year was only enough to hire back three of the seven assistants."

Leesa shook her head and said, "They didn't renew my contract at Oakview."

"Lee, you are the most dedicated teacher's assistant they ever had," I said. "I can't believe it."

"During the interview, one of the teachers on the committee asked me what I found most rewarding about my job," Leesa said. "I told them it was helping the children. As an example, I talked about helping little David read."

"I remember him," I said. "He had trouble in the beginning even sounding out the words. You invested your whole heart into him."

"I did. During the interview as I talked about that sweet little guy and remembered how he had excelled by the end of the year, I got all emotional and teared up."

"There's nothing wrong with that, Lee," I said. "It just shows how much you love those children."

"I don't want to weigh you down with all of this, Kev." She broke down and cried. "I so much wanted to stay as an aide where our girls attend school."

"It's going to be all right," I said. "We're going to hand this over to the Lord. We'll pray and just lean into Him."

I put my arms around her, and we stood awhile just holding each other.

Later we joined Mom and the girls in the visitation room and talked until we heard over the speaker that our time was up. As I stood up, Lindsey rushed toward me and locked her arms around my leg.

"Listen, honey," I said, trying to ease her grip, "your daddy has got to go back."

Lindsey screamed, "I don't want you to go!"

"Lindsey, let go of your daddy," Leesa said, trying to pull her back. "It's time to leave."

"I'll see you next Saturday," I said.

Finally, after Lindsey released my leg, I literally raced away so as not to hear her heartbreaking cry. With tears streaming down my cheeks, I hurried past inmates who stood watching the whole scene. When I got to my bed, I collapsed and sobbed. I felt utterly stripped. I remembered what Don had said about not thinking straight when you're upset and operating in the flesh. I still knew the Lord held me in the tender hollow of His hand, but at that moment I felt so helpless and even questioned my "assignment," as Don had called it.

The next day I was feeling a little better about Lindsey's outburst, knowing that Leesa was nearby to comfort her. I felt God's purpose behind it was for me to lean into Him and not let sadness defeat me. As true as this was, I soon saw that the Lord had used the upsetting moment with Lindsey for something even greater.

As I was walking toward the kitchen to work, Turbo was waiting for me. His usually expressionless eyes were damp with tears. He struggled to get his words out, his lower lip quivering.

"I've been watching you with your family, Kevin." He stopped talking and wiped his eyes. "I'll tell you this. When I get out of here, I'm going to be the world's best father to my kids."

I put my hand on his shoulder and said, "That's great, Turbo."

It was as if the Lord was taking all the unrelated experiences and stitching them together into one unique and colorful masterpiece.

"I love my kids," he said. "Who knows? Maybe my ex-wife and I could even work things out."

It was as if the Lord was taking all the unrelated experiences and stitching them together piece by piece, like a quilter sewing different scraps of cloth into one unique and colorful masterpiece.

CHAPTER

Thirteen

BY THE MIDDLE OF AUGUST, the Lord was already working a miracle for Leesa. Her friend Susie, a special education teacher at Oakview Elementary, was doing everything she could to locate a job for Leesa. She had even talked to her principal about getting funding and opening up a position for Leesa in the special education program.

Susie called her one day and said, "Good news: you're going to be an aide at the alternative school inside Verity Middle School."

In less than a week, Leesa was driving four blocks to help at a new school. She appreciated what Susie had done, and the opportunity, but she felt out of her element. She was used to working with elementary and not middle school children. Some of the students at the alternative school, many of whom had behavior problems, were bigger than Leesa.

And so we prayed that God would open a door at Oakview.

After one week at the alternative school, Leesa received another call from Susie.

"Guess what?" she asked. "You're back at Oakview! You'll be working with the special ed children."

It didn't take long for Leesa to fall in love with the children and, in turn, win their hearts. One boy named Michael referred to every color as "black," no matter how many times he was corrected. Leesa spent weeks holding up different-colored paper squares she had laminated, asking him repeatedly to identify their colors.

Holding up a red card, she'd ask, "What color are apples?" or, holding up a green card, "What color is grass?"

The boy kept saying, "Black."

When Michael gave the same answer about the white card, Leesa held it to her face and asked, "What color are my teeth?"

"Yellow," he said, and they laughed together.

To the delight of Michael's mother and grandmother, Leesa, over time, helped the boy learn to name colors, count numbers, and do simple math.

A letter from Leesa explaining all of this included one of my most treasured gifts: a picture of Lauren and Lindsey standing on our front porch.

Leesa had prompted them with, "Smile really big and show Daddy how happy you are going to your first day of school."

A photo of my daughters, Lindsey and Lauren, on their first day of school, which Leesa sent me while I was in prison.

Lauren had just had her bangs cut. She was smiling with her arm around her little sister. Both were wearing new shorts and T-shirts. The green-and-pink stripe across Lauren's navy front matched her sandals. Lindsey, also smiling and leaning into her sister, wore a pink top with two butterflies flitting across her middle. Her baby legs were so cute and chubby. Both girls wore brightly colored backpacks and held new lunch boxes.

Leesa sent me the photo so I wouldn't miss this precious moment.

In September, the warden moved me out of the kitchen to work in his office. I filed papers, vacuumed the floor, emptied the trash, and completed any number of tasks to assist him. My new position as aide extended to all of the administrative offices. Sometimes I was a runner, carrying supplies or delivering notes. Whatever was asked of me, I did my best to perform all my duties as for the Lord and not simply for my superiors.

I missed working with Benny in the kitchen, but he soon joined our Bible study group, and I saw him every day. He first came to our group out of curiosity, but after a few weeks, he committed his life to the Lord. Thereafter, he did his best to be near me at every meal or when the inmates were allowed in the compound. His thirst to learn more of God was never quenched, and so his questions were endless. I thought of Don's tender ways of mentoring me as I ministered to this young man.

One evening our group, now eleven members strong, spent the hour discussing how Noah's ark forecast God's provision for mankind through Jesus Christ. Benny listened quietly. He was forever the joker who enjoyed bantering playfully with anyone nearby, but rarely asked questions in a group setting. Instead, he was more comfortable catching me alone.

As I walked to breakfast the next morning, I felt someone tap my shoulder. When I turned, I saw it was Benny.

Without any kind of greeting, he launched directly into what had been weighing on his mind all night long. "What's all this ark and provision stuff?"

"Everything the Lord does has greater implications than what the naked eye can see," I said.

"Now, what does that mean?"

"The first chapter of Romans talks about the creation of the world being proof of God's eternal power and divine nature," I said. "So if you think about it, God didn't just create a physical world for us to live in. He also wanted the flowers, the trees, the ever-changing clouds to represent His handiwork and ultimately lure us into seeing Him."

"But what's that got to do with Noah and his ark?"

"The ark wasn't only a means to save Noah, his family, and all of the animals from the flood," I said. "God was also giving a tangible example of what He was going to do for everyone who enters into His divine plan."

"I still don't get it."

"Just as everyone inside the ark was saved, all those in Christ are saved," I said. "The ark symbolizes Christ."

Benny took hold of my arm to stop me in the compound. "Ah, come on, man," he said in disbelief. Then he got quiet, moving his eyes over the surrounding buildings and upward to the sky. Finally he released my arm and looked intently at me. "Man, that's amazing, isn't it?"

I smiled at his response. "It really is, Benny."

"I used to think the Lord was always just around the corner," he said, "but He's a lot closer than that; He's everywhere."

"I used to think the Lord was always just around the corner," he said, "but He's a lot closer than that; He's everywhere."

Over the next couple of months, more and more inmates either joined our group or started separate gatherings. It wasn't long before we had to split our group due to lack of space and little time to minister to each other. As I became closer to new inmates, I joined more Bible study meetings, which kept me busy every evening except Wednesdays and Sundays, when I attended the regular services organized by the prison chaplain. I didn't know whether someone had made a suggestion or if the chaplain had overheard me in one of the study groups, but I was asked to speak at those two services on a regular basis. There was no doubt in my mind, however, that the Lord was using not just me but many of the inmates to bring about a revival.

The chaplain was a good man who cared about the inmates, but he was inhibited in what he said due to government regulations, which forced him to tread lightly when it came to everyone's right to what he called "religious expression." I felt that at the very least I could offer the men passion for the Lord, because I knew firsthand how He was carrying me through the hardest years of my life. So when the chaplain asked me to serve on the Religious Service Council, I gladly accepted, hoping to make a difference.

The council included me, the chaplain, and a representative from the community of Manchester. Since I represented the institution, I always tried to keep the focus of our meeting on the needs of the inmates. We discussed how we could bring spiritual growth to the men through programs, events, and specific messages. It didn't take long to see how entangling all the regulations were regarding an inmate's freedom to worship. We were constantly strategizing how to submit to institutional policy and still meaningfully minister to the prisoners. As a government employee, the chaplain represented every faith. He struggled to give each religion its equal time and place to worship, while simultaneously following specific guidelines. Often religious demands became a power play between various groups not so much fighting for their religious rights as trying to outdo the opposing faiths.

I saw this conflict as a trap set by Satan to divert me and the other Christian men from God's divine purpose. Obviously, I believed Jesus' words about Himself. He said He is the way, the truth, and the life; no one can come to the Father except through Him. But this truth didn't motivate me to fight with other groups for the use of the prison's facilities. Instead, I discerned that wasting my time and energy in this kind of battle would impede the revival in our midst.

I made my convictions clear to the few men who were continually complaining to the chaplain. "I refuse to become engaged in all of these fights," I said. "Instead, I'm going to keep my focus on what the Lord wants me to do."

Some of them didn't appreciate my stance, but I didn't let that sway me. I refused to give in to something that I knew would obstruct the miracles that were taking place. And how could I explain the mounting revival that was overtaking the prison, except to say it was by the hand of God? The place was truly turning into something like an ongoing church retreat. Not every inmate embraced a new faith in Christ, but a great number of them did. Bible study

It became commonplace to see groups of men discussing the Bible, praying, or singing hymns.

meetings were springing up in every corner of the prison. It became commonplace to see groups of men discussing the Bible, praying, or singing hymns. It might be a gathering of three or twenty, but the Lord was bringing about something grand that I could hardly fathom.

I longed to be with my family, but at the same time, I felt a burden for the men I would be leaving in a few months. A number of them, especially Benny, sought me out for clarification of the Scriptures or for encouragement, just as I had done with Don. I was literally spending hours every week with these men. I got to know about their families, their pains, and their fears. The ones still harboring anger or struggling with depression concerned me the most, for they were setting themselves up to stay on their same dark track when placed back out on the street. All these men meant much more to me than I could ever have imagined. I had no idea when I first walked through the prison gate that the Lord would foster such friendships.

What gave me solace through my concerns was watching how another inmate named Brian exhibited a spiritual wisdom and natural tendency for leading the men. He had arrived a few months after me and would remain there about a year following my release. He was a new Christian and had an endless appetite for the Scriptures. When we sat across from each other at mealtimes, he usually had passages he wanted to discuss. It was a pleasure to share with him a number of truths that Don had taught me. Brian would pore over the verses and then find more connecting scriptures. With his brilliant mind, he learned quickly. He devoured the

Word of God not as a scholar seeking head knowledge but as a child yearning to know his Father.

One evening during a Bible study meeting, a man asked me to explain the curse of the law as described in the book of Galatians.

"Why don't you ask Brian?" I said. "See what insight he can give you."

He devoured the Word of God not as a scholar seeking head knowledge but as a child yearning to know his Father.

As I listened, Brian spoke in his usual gentle manner and explained how believers were freed from the curse of the law. I was now certain that the Lord was raising him to lead the inmates after I left.

As he shared his insights with other inmates, Brian used clear examples that every man present could understand. By the time he ended his explanation, everyone appeared to have a much clearer perspective on how to live in Christ's power.

From my observation of the men in the prison, it seemed the core of most of their problems was relying only on self. And most of their lives were marked by disappointment and defeat. The only way they knew to get what they wanted was through deceit and manipulation. Depending on the Lord to live through them was something most had never considered.

The men respected Brian and gravitated toward him. Over the following weeks, it became easier to send more and more men his way. It was obvious that this godly man could carry the ministry forward.

LAUREN WAS BECOMING a better reader and was drawn to anything with words, whether a book or a cereal box. One visiting day at Manchester when my mother and my sister, Karen, took the girls outside to play, Lauren became mesmerized by the sign at the front door that said FEDERAL BUREAU OF PRISONS.

She slowly pronounced the word "prisons" and then asked, "What does that mean?"

Lauren slowly pronounced the word "prisons" and then asked, "What does that mean?"

Mom and Karen looked at each other and didn't know what to say.

Then Karen quickly directed Lauren back to playing with her sister.

After the girls were inside the car and everyone was about to leave, Mom and Karen told Leesa. All three were devastated by the possibility that Lauren would soon understand what kind of place her father was in. In Lauren's and Lindsey's young minds, their father was being grounded at a sort of yearlong summer camp.

We were always honest with our daughters, but didn't want them prematurely exposed to what we knew they couldn't handle. Leesa and I continually prayed that the Lord would protect them from everything they saw and heard so they wouldn't be tarnished by the consequences of my wrongdoing. We knew our prayers were being answered when Leesa saw that the parents of Lauren's friends, as well as her teachers, never discussed my imprisonment with any of the children. No child ever asked Lauren about me and my situation. This was evidence of God's favor to us.

Leesa later told me about their drive home from the prison that day. As they drove toward a restaurant thirty miles away, Leesa, Mom, and Karen rode in silence with tears in their eyes. The thought of Lauren burdened with the full significance of this word broke them.

They were able, however, to put on happy faces for the girls while everyone ate lunch. Afterward, heading homeward with both Lauren and Lindsey asleep, they could talk freely.

"I just hate this," Mom said. "I hate for Lauren and Lindsey to be exposed to this sort of thing."

"I didn't know what to do, except to divert Lauren's attention to her sister," Karen said.

"It's all right," Leesa answered. "I know the Lord is protecting them, but Lauren is maturing so quickly and she's very curious. Someday both she and Lindsey will know the full truth. I wish we could keep this from them forever, but we just can't."

At her next visit, Leesa told me about this event piecemeal when the girls weren't in hearing distance.

During my incarceration and for some years following, Lauren would remain innocent about the meaning of the word *prison*. Much later, when both girls were old enough to understand, we openly discussed everything with them for the first time.

DURING DECEMBER, inmates received more visits from family and friends than they had all year long. Some of the mothers and wives came wearing red or green, sometimes displaying bright holiday pins on their blouses. One little girl had a tiny silver bell in her hair. I could tell by the animated expressions of the inmates that the entire month, with all of its holiday reminders, lifted their spirits. The sad part was seeing how, one by one, they sank after the departure of their guests.

Leesa had put red ribbons in Lauren's and Lindsey's hair. When I hugged them, I could smell the outdoors still clinging to their clothes.

"Right now I'm holding my two favorite Christmas gifts," I said.

"I should have wrapped them both up in big bows," Leesa said jokingly. I could tell she was in good spirits. She wore a bright-red sweater and couldn't have looked more beautiful. She seemed more relaxed than she had been in all of the previous visits.

"How are you doing, honey?" I asked.

"It has taken me a while," Leesa said, "but I'm starting to understand that I can trust the Lord to take care of all our needs."

"I'm doing fine," she said. "We miss you, but we're doing okay."

"Any trouble paying bills?"

"No. It's tight, of course, but we're making it."

"I know my parents are a great help," I said. "And Randy is just amazing to take over the house payments. I don't know how he can afford it."

"He got a second job," Leesa said. "I saw him one evening working at Pick 'n Save."

"What a great cousin and true friend."

"So is Bev," she said, referring to his wife. "Think of how much she and their children have to sacrifice with Randy being gone so much." Leesa took my hand and said, "It has taken me a while, but I'm starting to understand that I can trust the Lord to take care of all our needs."

"It has taken me a while to see a lot of things too."

Leesa told me her birth father, Robert, was also giving money and often dropped by the house to repair a running toilet or replace a broken light fixture. As she talked, I thought of him wearing his blue Dickies work pants, his shirt pocket overloaded with pens, while he pressed Leesa for something he could repair. He always enjoyed calling her Leesey Bug. Lauren was nicknamed "BG1," for being the baby girl born first, and Lindsey held the title of "BG2," for being the baby girl born second. He also attributed numbers to every little girlfriend of my daughters, each numbered consecutively, depending on the order in which he met them.

Leesa's father always amazed me with how he could work so efficiently while my girls pulled at his ball cap or fiddled with the tools he kept in a tackle box. Whenever Leesa caught Lauren and Lindsey hammering the wall or the edge of a door, she would tell them to stop bothering their grandfather.

Her father's answer was always, "Leave them alone, Leesey Bug. These are my two little workers."

After hearing Leesa tell how she appreciated family and friends, I agreed. "God has surrounded us with the best," I said.

"I think it's even more than the Lord just surrounding us with wonderful people," Leesa said. "I believe He is actively nudging everyone's hearts to help each other." She hesitated and then added, "It's hard to explain, much harder to comprehend."

"I know exactly what you mean," I said. "Sometimes people have shared a thought with me, not knowing how much I needed to hear it."

"Yes, and if the person couldn't know about your problem, it's a confirmation that the Lord is guiding them," Leesa said.

She told me about the time she'd balanced the checkbook after putting the girls to bed. She only had $7.56 left to last for the next two weeks. All she could do was pray. Two days later she received a card from one of our friends that included a check for $75. The next day as she stepped out of her car, our neighbor came across the driveway and handed her an envelope.

"I want to give this to you, and don't try to pay it back," she said. "This isn't a hardship to give, and I know the Lord wants me to do this. I just want to make sure that you have what you need."

They hugged each other and cried.

When Leesa went inside the house and opened the envelope, it was a card holding $500 in cash.

"Do you know what's more secure than having money?" Leesa asked me.

"What's that?"

"Trusting the Lord to take care of all our needs," she said.

I saw then the fullness of how Leesa was changing. She had faced so many obstacles and had endured so much, but she never gave up. She had remained faithful to me and her children, always following the Lord and keeping her sights on the future. Instead of allowing all the problems to destroy her and take her down, as Don had warned against, she chose to let them strengthen her. In so doing, she brought our family closer together.

I didn't really fully appreciate or even understand the process of the Lord's transformation until I was in prison. The environment and separation from my family magnified the importance of letting my troubles make me a better person. As strange as it may sound, my relationship with Leesa and my daughters became even closer during my incarceration.

On Thursday evening, February 10, 2000, as I was waiting for mail call with the other inmates, I was summoned over the intercom to go to the secretary's office. I assumed there had been some sort of spill or a delivery that needed immediate attention. When I walked into the office, the secretary was holding up a sheet of paper.

"I've got a real problem," she said.

"What's that?"

"I got a fax here saying you are to be released in six days." She waited a moment for the news to sink in and then smiled.

"I don't understand," I said. I was sure she had to have misread the fax. At the same time my mind was reeling with the possibility it was true. "Why are they releasing me four months early?"

"I got a fax here saying you are to be released in six days."

"I'm not sure," she said. "All I know is, I'm off tomorrow and we're facing a three-day weekend. This means I have only one day to process your release for Wednesday."

"This is a miracle."

"More than you know; they usually give me days to complete all the paperwork," she said. "You need to call your wife and tell her to pick you up Wednesday."

I called Leesa and said, "I'm coming home!"

By the next day, all the inmates knew I was leaving. They were genuinely happy for me, even those who had nothing to do with our prison ministry. As I talked to the men about my departure, the reality that I would probably never see any of them again began to sink in. I had gotten so close to some of them that I felt I knew the most significant individual in each man's life—the one he often thought about when he wanted to redirect his steps. It might be a grandmother who had told him Bible stories or a neighbor who had never stopped believing in him. Most of them reserved a soft place in their hearts for their mothers. Whenever one of the men abandoned his tough image and openly expressed regret over disappointing that special person, I knew he was taking a first step toward more good decisions to come.

It was terribly hard bidding these men farewell. Most difficult of all was saying good-bye to Benny. At first he didn't want to talk about it and hid behind his humor, saying, "Don't start too big of a revival out there; leave a little for me to do."

"I will, Benny."

He became quiet for a minute and then asked, "What am I going to do, Kevin? Who's going to tell me about the ark and using my talents and all that?"

"Brian is a wise man," I said. "You'll learn a lot from him."

"He'll be gone in a year," he said, hanging his head. "I'm stuck here for five more."

"The Lord will provide someone after him," I said. "Who knows, Benny, the next leader might be you."

He looked up at me and asked, "You think so?"

"Why not? Meditate on the Scriptures and let the Holy Spirit guide you and give you wisdom."

He smiled. "I'm glad you can go home, but I sure hate to see you leave."

"I'll miss you too, Benny."

Wednesday finally came. That morning I was told over the intercom to go to the office. I knew this meant that Leesa had just arrived and was ready to take me home.

I hurried down the long walkway toward the administrative building, but before I had even reached the halfway point, I was slowed down by inmates wishing me good luck. More and more men came out into the compound to bid me farewell.

The office paged me again and I continued my trek. The group of men walked with me, others joining. Just before I reached the back door, I turned and looked behind me. There were well over fifty men standing together, some smiling and a few teary-eyed. I knew each of them and had watched their lives change over the last few months. As they gathered there, I knew they were an example of how the Lord was prospering His Word and transforming all of us.

Standing taller than the rest, and crying, was Benny.

I lifted my hand to them and said, "I'll miss you guys. Love you all." I looked over each of their faces one last time and then turned to leave.

One of the most glorious sights of my life was Leesa sitting in the car, smiling as I came out the prison entrance. When I hugged her, I said, "Just think, we're no longer separated from each other."

"I've been counting off the days," she said. "So have the girls."

As Leesa drove us homeward, I must have asked a hundred questions about people I was excited to see again. She caught me up on Lauren and Lindsey, telling me how they were so excited for my return.

"It's going to be a little adjustment for Lauren and Lindsey,"

Leesa said. "I've been gently preparing them for sleeping in their own room again."

We both laughed about the girls camping out in the bedroom every night with Leesa.

"Have you heard anything about Don lately?" I asked.

"Randy told me that he's been sick with his diabetes," she said. "He has also been visiting his daughter in Columbus."

"He wrote me about his visits with his daughter, but he never mentioned being sick." Knowing Don as well as I did, I wasn't surprised that he would withhold such information. He was never one to draw attention to himself. I was certain that after I was home, I'd see him sometime between his visits with his daughter.

I should have been the happiest man in the world that afternoon as I moved farther and farther away from the prison, but I kept thinking about my friends still at Manchester. I didn't tell Leesa what I was thinking, but I grew silent as I thought about each man, considering his weaknesses and strengths, hoping each one would remain a faithful follower of Christ.

Knowing Don as well as I did, I wasn't surprised that he hadn't told me he was sick.

Just as Leesa had recognized my need to reflect quietly the day I was first sentenced, she could tell as she drove that this was another of those times.

As I pondered all this, God impressed upon me that carrying this kind of burden for all those men wasn't healthy. I needed to be focusing on what lay ahead for my family. I didn't have a job or even an idea for one, but I knew God would guide me. I had seen repeatedly throughout the last three years that He was always able to provide what was needed. Impossibilities didn't exist when it came to helping His children. If we earnestly seek answers from our heavenly Father, we never need to feel cornered or boxed in or trapped. He is always able to open up a way.

As Leesa and I headed homeward, I knew I had to release my worry concerning the future of the inmates. It was God who would take care of them. In fact, He had already raised Brian to mentor the men over the next year. And, of course, He would choose someone else after Brian. Neither I nor anyone else held everything together. Rather, it was Christ who actively transformed the lives of the believers. Those who hungered for the abundant life rested in the Lord and participated in this great plan.

With these thoughts, I trusted God to nurture my friends in Manchester, something He was already doing. And with every passing mile, I grew excited in anticipation of a new life with Leesa and my girls.

CHAPTER

Fourteen

LEESA AND I pulled up to our house and parked.

"Does this place look familiar to you?" Leesa said, smiling.

Before I had a chance to answer, Lauren and Lindsey came barreling out the front door. I stepped out of the car, and they both collided into my stomach, screaming for me to pick them up.

I lifted them to my chest and kissed them. "Your daddy has really missed you two."

"Carry us into the house," Lauren said.

"Both you girls have gotten so big. Your daddy will have to carry one and hold the hand of the other."

"Carry me," Lauren insisted.

"No," Lindsey said, "carry me."

"I'm going to be the one who picks," Leesa said. "Lindsey's the smallest, so she can be carried; Lauren can hold Daddy's hand."

When we walked into the house, I saw that it was full of family and friends. I hugged Mom and Karen first, and then my brother-in-law. Sadly, my father wasn't present because he was on the job that day. I know my father and the love he has for his children, so I feel his absence had more to do with wanting to see me one-on-one after my release. I wondered if he feared he would be overtaken with emotion in front of others when he saw me.

"Welcome home, honey," Mom said.

She and Karen were teary-eyed, but not as much as me. I was overwhelmed with joy to see everyone. I knew I was looking into the faces of family and friends who really cared about me, Leesa, and our girls. I was beholding a group of people who had stayed with us through it all. My sin and public humiliation hadn't deterred any of them from standing with me.

My sin and public humiliation hadn't deterred any of my friends and family from standing with me.

Pastor Chuck and Jamie presented me with a pizza.

"We know you've been missing this for some time," Pastor Chuck said with a big grin.

"I sure have," I said, and everyone laughed.

This homecoming couldn't have been better. My friends from the church Bible study group were also present. They each expressed their happiness at my return, commenting on how Leesa, the girls, and I made such a beautiful family. It was hard to control my tears as I listened to their sweet words.

After a short while, everyone said their good-byes so I could be alone with Leesa and the girls. With Lauren and Lindsey still hanging on to me, I waved to everyone as they drove off.

"I can hardly believe it," I said to Leesa. "Am I really home?"

"Yes, you are," she said. "You're home to stay."

THE NEXT DAY I went to see Pastor Chuck and Jamie to inquire about leads they might have for a job. I wasn't asking them for work, but just wanted a name or an available position that I could pursue. I told them I would be happy to find anything to support my family.

The Lawrences put me in touch with Mike and Cathy, a couple in the church who owned a telecommunications business. I immediately felt a connection with them when they interviewed me the next day. I knew it was another blessing from the Lord when they hired me to work in their office. Their graciousness created the kind of environment that encouraged people to use their gifts and talents in their workplace.

Not long after my release, the woman who had taken over the grocery store had gone out of business, and ultimately, I sold the building. In the end, the money made on the sale barely paid off the loan. During this time, Leesa, the girls, and I were becoming more involved at Christ Temple Church. I volunteered to do whatever was needed, whether it was putting up tables and chairs for meetings or cleaning up after fellowship dinners. I'd had a lot of practice at Manchester.

Eventually I became the "vital link" team leader and oversaw various ministry teams that connected people to the church. This new position was much more demanding, but I enjoyed every aspect of it, knowing the Lord had prepared me for this. I could also sense that He was using this period to lay the foundation for what lay ahead.

RANDY TOLD ME that Don was visiting his daughter in Columbus more and more. He knew this through his mother, who lived in the high-rise.

"Is he getting sicker?" I asked.

"I'm not sure if he's worse," Randy said. "I do know he's had real trouble with his diabetes since you've been gone."

"I have a new cell phone and don't have his number in my contacts," I said. "When I've tried calling what I thought was his number, I was never sure whether I was dialing the wrong number or he just wasn't answering."

"You probably called when he was with his daughter."

I called Velma to see what she knew. "Don is much sicker," she said. "He's been living with his daughter for several months at a time."

"Does he still come back into town?"

"Don is much sicker," Velma said. "He's been living with his daughter for several months at a time."

"I think so," she said. "He still has his place at the high-rise."

I told her about changing cell phones, but explained that Don could still reach me using my old number. "He knows through my letters that I'm out of prison now," I said. "I don't understand why he hasn't tried to contact me."

"You know how he is," she said. "He's very private and never wants to impose on you or your family."

Don with his daughter, Donita Toney Rossiter, whom he lived with in his last few years.

"I'd like to see him."

"Call him," she said. After giving me his daughter's number, she added, "I'm sure he wants to hear from you."

I didn't know what Don had told his daughter about me. He had told me very little about her. And because he had often diverted my attempts to meet her when she visited Ironton, I was hesitant to call. I didn't know how his daughter would receive someone fresh out of prison trying to contact her sick father. I longed to talk to my friend, but I didn't want to place an unneeded burden on him in his present state.

With these concerns, I finally called that evening and asked if Don was there.

"Yes, Daddy's here," his daughter said.

I explained that Don had worked for me at the store, but I was careful not to overemphasize our friendship.

"Oh, yes," she said. "He mentioned that he made deliveries for the corner store in Ironton."

I quickly discerned that Don hadn't shared much about me with his daughter. I knew then that it was best not to ask to talk to him. "I just wanted to call to make sure that he's okay," I said.

"He's having a hard time, but he's going to be all right."

After I thanked her and got off the phone, I felt I shouldn't have called. I had wanted to check on Don, but I hadn't learned anything new. Besides, Don knew I was now out of prison and could have contacted me at the same number he had used many times in the past. In the end, I concluded that I needed to accept Don's way of guarding his family and allow him the freedom to call me when he wanted. This made me sad, but it seemed to be the right decision.

One Monday morning as I was driving to work, the Lord told me to tell Pastor Chuck Lawrence that whatever he was doing, I was also supposed to do. These words were not audible, but they came to me with the kind of clarity and authority that only comes from God.

After I arrived at work, I told Cathy about my experience.

"If the Lord told you this, you had better do it," she said.

I agreed, and made an appointment to meet with Pastor Chuck the next day.

Later that afternoon, Mike asked me to accompany him on a business trip to Florida the next day, when I was supposed to have my appointment with Pastor Chuck. Since I would be coming back on Wednesday, I called the church and rescheduled to meet Pastor Chuck the day after I returned.

As I arrived at Christ Temple Church on Thursday, I saw Pastor Chuck and Jamie in the parking lot and walked inside with them. After Jamie went into the office, Pastor Chuck led me into the nursery room for a private conversation.

> **I concluded that I needed to accept Don's way of guarding his family and allow him the freedom to call me when he wanted.**

Pastor Chuck inquired about Leesa and the girls, and then asked, "What can I do for you, Kevin?"

"I don't know what this means," I said, "but the Lord told me that whatever you are doing, I am also supposed to do."

Pastor Chuck stopped smiling and stared at me until tears streamed down his face. I was taken aback, thinking that this man was overly sensitive.

"Do you know what you're asking?"

"No," I said, "I don't."

He told me about the tremendous struggles he was facing as he worked to grow this new church. He knew that what he was doing was God's plan, but he was facing many obstacles. The battles weren't only financial; he was also dealing with a number of people who were opposed to the new church building built—including some influential neighbors and city council members.

"Last night Jamie said we should ask the Lord to send me someone to help." He expressed his thankfulness for his wife's ongoing faithfulness and self-sacrifice, but told me they'd agreed that he needed another man to partner with him in this uphill battle.

I was struck by the fact that my rescheduled appointment had followed their prayer perfectly. "I'm the one to partner with you," I said.

"I'm only going to eat one meal a day until the church building is completed," he said. "You can join me."

"The Lord said that whatever you are doing, I am supposed to do too."

"The Lord said that whatever you are doing, I am supposed to do too," I said.

We began this unusual fast together, and continued it for thirteen months until the building was completed—debt-free. Through this period of trials and battles, Pastor Chuck and I became closer than brothers.

In 2002 I began serving as the executive pastor, and my schedule became much busier. About a year later I was interviewed on a local Christian TV broadcast. I shared that the Word of God pointed the way to Christ. "Jesus," I told the host, "is revealed from cover to cover, from Genesis to Revelation." The passages I quoted as proof were the very scriptures Don had taught me and that were now a part of me.

As I left the studio and started toward my car, my cell phone rang. When I took it out and read the number, I immediately recognized that it was Don calling.

I was surprised by Don's voice. It was obvious that his health was failing. He was coughing more than ever, and he sounded much weaker. He said he still had his place at the high-rise, but wasn't going to keep it.

"I watched you on the broadcast, son," Don said. "The student has now become the teacher."

"I'm really sick, son," he said. "I'm going to live permanently with my daughter."

"I'm sure she's glad that you can be together," I said. "Columbus isn't very far; I'd love to come visit sometime."

After a long silence, he said, "I watched you on the broadcast, son. The student has now become the teacher."

It took me three years of working and raising money to make restitution with the bank. The executives were surprised that I offered this, since the judge had dismissed the civil suit, but I explained that it was the right thing to do. When I read the Bible story about Zacchaeus, the chief tax collector whom Jesus talked with, and that he paid back all those he had defrauded, I knew I needed to follow his example. I couldn't let my wrongdoing pass without making some kind of amends.

On February 11, 2008, Velma called to tell me that Don had passed away the day before, on Sunday. It was difficult for her to talk through her crying.

"He was a lovely man," she said.

"Yes, he was."

"Have you talked with him lately?"

"No, Velma. Ever since he permanently moved in with his daughter, I decided to let him call when he wanted." I paused and then added, "I hope that was the best approach for him."

"I think it was," she said. "He was a sweet man, but he had his own way of doing things. Maybe he felt that the Lord had fulfilled His purpose in your friendship, and it was time to let you go."

> **"Maybe he felt that the Lord had fulfilled His purpose in your friendship, and it was time to let you go."**

I thought about Don's last words to me on the day I came out of the TV studio. "Yes," I said. "You're probably right."

Velma told me the family was going to have Don's funeral service at the City Mission Church in Ironton, where Don's friends attended. His body was going to be transported the 120 miles from Columbus.

I couldn't think of Don as being gone. He was always in my thoughts. His soft demeanor and compassionate words were as real to me that evening as they had been eleven years earlier when he and I had first met. What he taught me had transformed my view of everything, because he showed me the true person of Jesus Christ.

Before I shared the news with Leesa, I spent a few minutes alone praying and mourning the loss of my good friend.

THE DAY OF DON'S FUNERAL came during one of the worst snowstorms I had ever seen. Matt, the Christian education team leader at Christ Temple Church, joined me, and we drove slowly across the bridge and through the streets of Ironton. The only activity we saw en route was a truck plowing an open path on the opposite side of the road.

The City Mission Church was a beautiful sight to behold. The blanket of snow that covered the steps and rested in the crook of the steeple accentuated the bright redbrick front. As I drove closer, I saw that there were no cars in the parking lot.

"Why don't you wait in the car," I said to Matt, "until I make sure what's happening."

I went up the steps and found a note on the door. The writing was a little messy, as if someone with cold, numb fingers had hurriedly written the message.

The note said:

> The funeral for Don Toney has been rescheduled due to inclement weather. The family and funeral director were unable to make the trip. It is postponed until further notice.

The next day, I searched the obituaries for information about Don's funeral service, but found nothing. I was certain they wouldn't transport his body on this day because the weather was even worse.

The following day, I called the church. To my dismay, I had missed the funeral. Despite the heavier snowfall of the previous day, they had brought his body to Ironton, and then buried him across the border in Wurtland, Kentucky, where his brother had given him a cemetery plot.

He had entered my life quietly and with timidity. And that's how he left, silently and unassumingly.

At first I was devastated, because I had wanted to honor Don by attending his funeral. But then, as I thought about it, I realized how this situation was so representative of Don and his private ways. He had entered my life quietly, with the timidity of a man who never wanted to impose himself on anyone. And that's how he left, silently and unassumingly.

Don's headstone, in Wurtland, Kentucky.

On that cool day in March 1997, I had no idea what treasures lay inside that gentle stranger dressed in shabby clothes, who surprised me with the statement "Jesus is revealed from cover to cover, from Genesis to Revelation." It seemed a lifetime ago that I had watched him turn the pages of my Bible to prove those words.

His friendship changed my life, and I believe that our friendship changed his life as well. He showed me the significance of the story about Jesus washing the disciples' feet. When Peter resisted this act of servitude, the Lord said Peter would have no part with Him if he refused. Although Don never got around to expounding on this passage, all of his teaching taught me its meaning: that I must allow Jesus to serve me before I can serve Him. We love the Lord only because He first loved us. This is grace. Once I allowed the Lord to reveal Himself and minister to me, I was then able to minister to others. This transformed my view of God and people and even money. The more I learned of the Lord, the more I loved Him. I learned that He views me as His child, and He lavishes me with abounding love and tenderness.

I had learned this and much more from a broken man whose compassion overrode all his personal heartaches, a man who spilled out his love liberally on anyone who accepted it. The Lord had sent Don to me at a time when I, too, was broken. My sin had forced me and my family into a very dark place. It was Don, however, who showed me that the Lord wanted to restore us and bring us into the light. For me, being with Don at the store during those two years was much like resting in the eye of a storm. Whenever I was consumed with worry about finances or imprisonment or the welfare of my family, he always provided a quiet atmosphere, untouched by everything outside of us. I soon learned through him that most of the storm that hung about me was of my own creation. Some days, the frustration and confusion seemed to overwhelm me, but then, I would find myself sitting quietly at the counter, once again comforted by my friend.

Don cried over the beauty and truth of God's Word, and he laughed heartily over something as simple as a child discarding a candy wrapper.

Don cried over the beauty and truth of God's Word, and he laughed heartily over something as simple as a child discarding a candy wrapper. Watching him enjoy what most would find insignificant gave me insight into how much our heavenly Father takes pleasure in us.

Don had instilled much more in me than he ever knew. Because he revealed to me the true Christ, the One Who loves and restores broken lives, my marriage has continued to become stronger with every passing year. His mentoring has blessed not only my relationship with Lauren and Lindsey, but also the lives of my youngest daughter, Lakyn, and my son, Kaiden, whom Don never met.

Now when I hold my granddaughters, Braylie and Aubree, I count the days until I can tell them, as I have my two youngest children, about my dear friend whom the Lord sent me, years earlier one bright March morning. And if I can tell the story well enough, maybe they, and others, will learn to look past the outer appearance of strangers and know the intrinsic value the Lord has placed in all of us.

ACKNOWLEDGMENTS

KEVIN WEST: I owe a debt of gratitude to my dear friend Don, whose friendship changed my life forever. During the creation of this book, I spent over two years retracing all that had transpired throughout our relationship. I couldn't include everything about this extraordinary person. If I had, it would fill too many pages. And so this project became a process of recalling and selecting the best details which would successfully convey Don and the struggles we endured together.

ACKNOWLEDGMENTS

I thank my wife, Leesa, for loving me and our children and grandchildren with such an abounding love that never ceases.

I thank my daughters, Lauren, Lindsey, and Lakyn; my son, Kaiden; my granddaughters, Braylie and Aubree; and my son-in-law, Bradley, who is married to Lauren—who will always be the lights of my life.

I will forever be indebted to my parents, Paul and Pat West, and my sister and brother-in-law, Karen and Robin Arthur, for their many sacrifices and loving encouragement.

I am also grateful to my in-laws, Robert Whitt and Betty Whitt Paholsky, for their love and support.

I thank Randy Taylor for his selfless generosity. I also want to thank his wife, Bev, and his daughter, Tiffany, for their giving in every area.

I deeply appreciate my agent, Les Stobbe, who encouraged the writing of this story. I appreciate his business savvy and insight.

I am grateful to Philis Boultinghouse for all her work on this project. She is an incredibly gifted editor.

I want to thank Katie Sandell and everyone at Howard Books who worked diligently on this project.

A special thanks to John Frederick Edwards, my writing partner and friend, for his gift of long-suffering and storytelling, as well as his skill of probing me with a thousand questions.

I also want to thank Don's children.

ACKNOWLEDGMENTS

JOHN FREDERICK EDWARDS: I want to thank Kevin West for his friendship and for his partnership in what has become an incredible journey. I also want to thank Les Stobbe, the king of agents, who has taught me much about the publishing business. I thank Philis Boultinghouse, Senior Editor, whose editing skills can only be described as God-given. Working with her has enriched my writing. I greatly appreciate Katie Sandell's expert assistance, Joal Hetherington's copyediting skills, and the dedicated team at Howard Books. I also want to thank Ruth McDonald and Amber Johnson for their encouragement. I especially thank my beloved wife, Janet, who never wavered in her love or her belief in me. How is it possible that I can have a beautiful wife, faithful friend, and gifted editor all in one person?

In loving memory of my good friend Don. Without him, there would be no story.